Blind Spot

Published by 404 Ink Limited
www.404Ink.com
@404Ink

Editing: Heather McDaid
Typesetting: Laura Jones
Cover design: Luke Bird
Co-founders and publishers of 404 Ink: Heather McDaid & Laura Jones

Print ISBN: 978-1-912489-42-8
Ebook ISBN: 978-1-912489-43-5

Printed and bound in Great Britain by Clays Ltd, Elcograf S.p.A.

LOTTERY FUNDED

404 Ink acknowledges support for this title from
Creative Scotland via the Crowdmatch initiative.

Blind Spot

Exploring and Educating on Blindness

Maud Rowell

Inklings

Contents

Author's note

Throughout this book, I have used the terms "blind" and "blindness" to encompass a diverse spectrum of non-normative ways of seeing that cannot be corrected; I have only used terms like partially sighted or visually impaired when quoting someone else. The reason for this is purely personal – I do not wish for my vocabulary to feel clinical or medical, or categorise people unnecessarily. It is not that I take offence from alternative terms – it is simply that I identify as blind, and so this is the word I choose to use. I also think rehabilitating the word "blind" to refer to all of these ways of seeing helps people better understand that blindness, by its very nature, is spectral – it is not just one thing. We should embrace that it has a multitude of meanings, and manifests itself in different ways for everyone.

Everyone I spoke to directly is referred to with their given name after being introduced; Japanese and Korean names are written with their family name first and given name second.

Introduction

"Are you human?"

This question floats in the middle of my computer screen, accompanied by a gridded image on which I am instructed to pick out all the traffic lights, motor-bikes, or taxis. It's a common enough dialogue box to encounter on the web – a way for one machine to determine whether or not it's interacting with another. Ever the shapeshifter, it has previously greeted me in the form of a string of shadowy letters printed in a wavy, obtuse pattern inside a pale grey rectangle, which I must transcribe. Easy enough – if you can see. The problem is that I can't.

There is a small icon to indicate that I can switch the cue to an audio one. But the visual cue always comes first, and the audio is always the alternative, the deviation from the norm. The question my computer is asking reminds me that among those for whom this test is designed to be simple, I am atypical.

For the majority of the human race, sight is the primary sense: it is how we chiefly perceive, build, navigate, and describe the world around us. The very origin of the sense was a game-changer. It first appeared in now-extinct trilobites 541 million years ago, triggered an evolutionary arms race, and ushered in a golden age of biological innovation known as the Cambrian Explosion.[1] Almost every animal in existence today can trace its ancestry back to this flourishing catalysed by the organic camera, humans included.

Visual information is so important to our brains that it can even override other kinds of sensory intel, literally altering reality as we perceive it. In a phenomenon known as the McGurk effect, for example, when we see a video clip of someone's mouth pronouncing the syllable "fa", that is the sound we hear, even if the overlaid audio is of the syllable "ba". Our brains trust our eyes so much that they overwrite what our ears are telling us. Our reliance on sight is also the reason so many of us are afraid of the dark: the complete lack of visual stimuli is such an extreme sensory deprivation for humans that an ancient, obsolete anxiety creeps in, and our imaginations fill the unknowable black void with danger. Horror films capitalise off this instinct all the time.

As the visual system is our primary sensory organ, fear of blindness is extremely prevalent. In one 2016 study,

2,044 American adults were asked what the worst disease that could happen to them would be: blindness was the highest ranked answer nationally, having been selected as either the first or second worst case scenario by all subgroups of respondent.[2]

In another study conducted in the Indian state of Andhra Pradesh in 2002, researchers found that blindness was – again – the disability that was feared the most (it was selected by 92% of respondents, with paralysis coming in second).[3] This study also asked its 10,293 participants to say whether or not they agreed with the following statements: 1) blind people have to depend on sighted people to do most of their things; 2) blind people can never really be happy; 3) not much should be expected from blind people; and 4) losing one's sight means losing one's self. Across every subgroup, at least 70% of respondents agreed with every single statement; in most cases, more than 90% agreed.

For the first 19 years of my life, when I could see, I had no cause to think about whether or not I agreed or disagreed with those statements myself. I had never encountered anybody blind, and I only saw one-dimensional stereotypes or clichés of blind people in the media and in pop culture – certainly no one to whom I could relate. Blindness (as a concept, a social issue, a reality) floated far away from the edge of my own consciousness, something abstract and intangible. It may as well have been pulled from the world of fantasy or fiction. If I'd interrogated myself, I'm sure I would have envisaged blindness as like being enveloped in pure blackness, as many others do. It's the "darkness which the blind do see" after all, as Shakespeare wrote in his 27th sonnet.

Then, one hot June night in Seoul, South Korea, as I was finishing up a year of travelling and working before beginning my undergraduate degree, I realised quite suddenly that people's faces had become invisible. Or rather, there was a kind of shimmering hole in the middle of my vision, so that when I looked directly at something, it was eaten up by that fuliginous central lacuna.

I took myself to hospital, and underwent days of tests, without conclusive answers. Then I was taken in for the first of many eye injections. No one explained the procedure to me, so I lay on the gurney staring up at impossibly bright lights, fighting the panic that was rising in my throat like vomit. The needle went in, and was withdrawn again, and after that the surgeon told me – as I wore my clear plastic eyepatch, feeling fragile and self-conscious – that I had a rare, degenerative eye disease that would make me blind. The injection had not been to cure a small medical blip that could soon be forgotten, as I'd hoped. Rather, it was the beginning of my new life, with a disability that wasn't static, but something requiring regular trips to hospital and eye injections every four to eight weeks, potentially forever, to try and slow inevitable degeneration down.

Going blind myself, I found that a part of me really did feel that losing one's sight means losing one's self. I was the girl who was always reading books, writing stories, drawing and painting. If I had to sacrifice those aspects of myself, what would be left? If I couldn't see, who was I? Blindness had floated towards me out of the ether, and now it touched every single aspect of my life. And the loss of my sensory comfort zone alone was terrifying – but so too was the harmful narrative surrounding disability I unearthed inside myself. This toxic thinking now applied to me as well as to a whole community that had suddenly stopped being invisible, because now I was looking for it.

So much of that internalised negativity stemmed from ignorance. Without knowing about how blind people engage with the world, I was unable to picture my own future and think strategically about the changes that lay ahead. Without understanding that blindness could manifest itself in the way it did for me – slowly losing my central vision over years – I was completely unprepared for the grieving process that I had to go through. And without being aware of the many brilliant blind people in the world today and throughout history, I struggled to conjure examples of people who proved that the blind really could be independent, and successful, and happy, and realise their ambitions without sight loss limiting them.

But humans can excel without sight, as countless examples prove. Blind people have given us some of the world's greatest and most culturally significant works of literature, art, and music. They have climbed Everest and won Masterchef. They have revolutionised the mathematical realm, redefined language, and developed our understanding of the solar system and of our oceans. And they have driven – and continue to drive – innovation in almost every field, because seeing differently engenders extraordinary creativity in the realm of problem-solving. Blind people think outside the box that most of us spend our lives in, and we can all harness and benefit from this, in terms of intellectual progress and social justice alike.

So while sight loss will always be an adjustment, it should never mean a severing from your sense of self, or from happiness – and we shouldn't think it does, either. No one should have to feel that should they go blind, they must sacrifice their dreams or independence. We must fight the pervasive ignorance which feeds this mindset, and which continues to relegate blind history, blind accomplishments, and the realities of sight loss to the shadows. Doing so is a crucial step towards us all becoming better, more tolerant and empathetic members of diverse global communities, and towards making our world more equal, more creative, and more accommodating of difference.

So let's start with the basics. What is blindness, what does it look like – and why does knowing this matter?

Shakespeare, and so many others, are wrong: it's actually rare to see nothing but the colour black. Blindness is a spectrum, and can take many forms (and most contrary to the popular imagination, people who have had their eyes removed see a kind of white fog). The Argentinian writer Jorge Luis Borges (1899-1986) sought to dispel this myth, stating in a 1977 lecture: "The world of the blind is not the night that people imagine."[4] For Borges, pure darkness was even one of the things he could no longer perceive, and he spent a long time struggling to sleep after the night became characterised by a "greenish or bluish mist, vaguely luminous".[5]

One tangible effect of this lack of awareness of a low vision spectrum is the fact that blind people face accusations of faking their impairment, because they contradict the popular image of someone with their disability. That Stevie Wonder is only pretending to be blind has been a popular conspiracy theory for years.[6] It's not just celebrities who catalyse these rumours: a photo taken without consent of a blind woman holding a cane in one hand and a smartphone in the other went viral on Facebook in January 2019, and she was voraciously denounced as a fraud by the online community.[7] This is no isolated incident: blind people often have to justify their disability to uninformed strangers, and I have certainly had to engage in this emotionally exhausting practice on many an occasion.

Clearly, a lack of awareness is not a neutral position to take, or an apathetic one: it can inflict palpable damage, and we are passing it on from one generation to another. According to one UK study from 2015, 43% of blind children had been bullied at school, and their parents believed education about sight loss can play a key role in ending this abuse.[8] Only 15% of parents with a blind child felt that other parents were presenting their own sighted children with a positive role model for how to interact with the blind – but 91% felt that educating these parents would help change the way their sighted children treated their blind classmates.

Ignorance also begets inaction, because you can't act on knowledge that you do not have. Without knowing about the realities of sight loss, people don't factor accessibility into how they create culture, interact socially, or design environments, objects and infrastructure. This perpetuates a cycle of injustice on a much larger scale. Every book that is not released in an accessible format, every museum which excludes the blind from engaging with their own history and heritage through artefacts, every city which can only be explored safely and independently if you can see, increases the gap between those who have sight and those who don't. How can we expect great things from blind people when we don't grant them the same access to so many of the things which educate us, give us pleasure, or make us human?

There are also layers of injustice at play here, because blindness does not affect everybody equally, even though it can affect anybody. Globally, more women than men experience blindness (in the UK, two thirds of people living with sight loss are women), and certain ethnic groups are significantly more at risk of some of the leading causes of blindness than others.[9] Black African and Caribbean people are four to eight times more likely to contract glaucoma, and among the South Asian community, diabetic eye disease is three times more prevalent.[10]

It's also lower-income countries and communities that are more acutely affected. In the UK, the leading causes of blindness are diseases for which there are currently no cures – but worldwide, 80% of all sight loss is preventable, and the issue becomes access to healthcare.[11] Perhaps the most telling demonstration of this imbalance is the fact that even though cataracts can be removed in a 15-minute outpatient procedure in many parts of the world, they are still the leading cause of blindness in low and middle income countries. To date, over 65 million people worldwide are blind due to cataracts.[12] So for each aspect of our lives that is inaccessible to the blind, we exacerbate pre-existing problems of inequality, granting more privilege to those who already have it.

But it's not enough just to think about blindness as a medical issue, something to be cured and fixed – because that negates the value of vast numbers of people around the world who live with it unavoidably. These large groups of people aren't going away, because despite global efforts, blindness is still on the rise. According to the Royal National Institute of Blind People (RNIB), there are roughly 2 million people living with sight loss in the UK, and this number is set to double by 2050.[13] The RNIB also tells us that someone begins losing their sight every six minutes. That's 250 people every day.

Those are some big numbers, and hiding behind them are real people, who upon going blind must take on the emotional weight of the negativity we all unconsciously internalise about disability. The way we think about blindness matters. We must all fight the mindset that sight loss makes us less than our sighted counterparts, because if we truly believe the blind cannot accomplish greatness, or have no social utility, or are not as good as those with sight, then we make those statements true. It's a self-fulfilling prophecy that we all have the power to break.

Blind Spot will, I hope, help in some small way to do just that. Its collection of essays shines a light on how blindness intersects with a multitude of topics – from environment and infrastructure to science and technology, and from human innovation to pop culture and the arts. While it is packed with data, it was important to me that this book be full of the voices of real people who exist behind the screen of numbers and statistics. Brilliant blind voices from all around the world – from Italy to Mali, the United States to South Korea – fill these pages, spanning many fields: computer science, world music, astronomy, painting and more. They have all accomplished remarkable things, not in spite of being disabled – which does not cap one's ability to achieve greatness – but in spite of a disabling world and the disabling mindsets that still fill it.

I truly believe there is value in learning about blindness for everyone, because making our world more accessible benefits all its citizens, not just the few for whom it is critical. And by reconfiguring how we conceptualise blindness, we can all be better and kinder people, and reduce the trauma of sight loss for those who experience it, both now and in the future.

I encourage you not to expect less from the blind, but to expect more from our environments, our leaders, and our ways of teaching and learning and thinking. Engage critically with the systems that surround us all, from the big – like how race, gender and class intersect with blindness – all the way down to the mundane and everyday, like a simple robotic test asking: "Are you human?"

Chapter 1:
On visibility

For a time, I only ate food that had been wrapped in plastic. Only when a voluminous pile of shiny, transparent waste had accumulated beside me, and I had unsheathed a fresh pair of disposable chopsticks, did I know that it was safe. All that glossy plastic was what made it so: I knew everything it covered was guaranteed hygienic and untouched. Its sheen protected me, prevented me from poisoning myself with dirt.

It was the spring of 2018, and I was living in a student dormitory in Kyoto. Outside the window were black butterflies as big as my hand, and mountains that looked overrun with spirits when the clouds came down. There were magic purple sunsets that lasted mere minutes, when the sky blazed neon violet above a city sparkling like out-of-focus sequins, half-buried in crepuscular haze. But to me, the most beautiful place in the world had become the inside of a convenience store. Those sterile white spaces – reliably posted on every street corner in Japan – were safe havens, with their identical aisles of plastic-wrapped food and cleaning products, and mollifying instrumental covers of Abba songs or *Cheer Up, Sleepy Jean*.

This version of myself was one I had never seen before, and never imagined becoming. Anxiety over cleanliness was infecting my personality and body as I watched, powerless to intervene, as though from behind a two-way mirror I could never hope to shatter. Outside my door was a whole world of things the old me wanted to explore, and this pale shadow of myself was wasting it all, gobbling up all my time, energy, and willpower. In the shower, dark skeins of hair came away in my fingers. I lost weight. I got anaemic. I sanitised my hands, over and over and over, until my palms cracked like deserts.

It was sight loss that was taking such a toll on my health. My vision was deteriorating faster than ever before. The shimmering hole in the centre of my field of view was making everything look like it was crawling with insects – so how could I tell if something was dirty or clean? I could only know for sure if I pulled off the plastic myself. Doing so also helped me take back some semblance of control, because even though I was making six-hour round trips to an Osaka hospital for eye injections each month, the degeneration showed no signs of slowing down. Then, on top of everything else, the anaesthetic stopped working.

The links between blindness and poor mental health are well established. In the UK, more than four in 10 people attending a low vision clinic are suffering with symptoms of clinical depression, and 31% of blind people are rarely or never optimistic about the future.[1] Four in every ten blind people also feel moderately or completely cut off from people and things around them.[2] The RNIB website catalogues a whole host of recognised emotional responses sight loss can trigger – including grief, depression, fear, anger, and denial – and notes that a loss of identity and subsequent renewal of one's sense of self are essentially part and parcel of the experience.[3] Yet emotional support structures for the community are significantly lacking – only 17% of people experiencing sight loss are offered services like therapy or counselling, even though two thirds of those of working age reported that they would have wanted it, had it been available.[4]

A community is suffering – and visibility is a key part of the problem.

The worst aspect of the mental health crisis I experienced in Japan was that I felt alone. I didn't have any blind mentors or role models; nor did I see any relatable blind characters in pop culture. This sparked intense feelings of isolation on a level I had never known existed. For the first time, I was able to recognise the gaps in our education systems, media, and the curation of our collective memories – gaps which block everyone from engaging with blindness in a healthy, productive way, both emotionally and intellectually. I realised that having a robust, resilient sense of self is linked to how validated we feel by society; when that validation is lacking, we have to work that much harder to love and believe in ourselves. In Japan, because blind people had been hidden from me my whole life, I had to try and champion myself in an information and inspiration vacuum. And it was exhausting, and made my mind and body sick.

Amadou Bagayoko – one half of blind musical duo and real-life married couple Amadou & Mariam – expounded to me on the importance of people being able to see and learn from the visibility of blind people. "When you are blind, you find yourself in a world where the sighted majority don't understand your reality," he said. "It is essential to have examples like Ray Charles and Stevie Wonder in life, so that both sighted and blind people have references. For the sighted, these people bring us closer together and allow us to show our reality, and for the blind, they serve as an inspiration. From the moment a blind person sees a role model just like them, doing things, overcoming goals, that person gives them the courage and example to move forward."

I wish, for instance, that at my lowest points I had known about Lieutenant James Holman (1786-1857), who now sits at the very top of my personal pantheon of heroines and heroes. Holman was completely blind: he lost his sight in his mid-twenties, quite suddenly, after chronic rheumatism had ended his career in the British Royal Navy, stranding him forever a lieutenant. He was also the world's greatest premodern traveller – a man who, by the end of his extraordinary life, had made a journey of around 250,000 miles – a distance roughly equal to that between the Earth and the moon.[5]

Holman navigated every conceivable terrain, from the frozen wastes of Siberia (then a dreaded penal colony) to deserts; he slogged through malarial jungles, waded through swamps, and climbed volcanoes. He rode mules through the Brazilian rainforest, which was so dense it was navigable only by lighting great mile-long swathes of foliage on fire.[6] When he wasn't flanked by the sensory chaos of flames (as deafening as "contending armies in the din of battle", he tells us), lurking swarms of wasps would – on occasion – explode out from the trees in dark, horrifying thunderheads.[7]

His list of accomplishments doesn't end there. He trained as a doctor, fought slavery in Equatorial Guinea, committed many of the world's great literary master-pieces to memory, learned various languages, and contributed to the global bank of knowledge with several meticulously researched accounts of his travels. One of these was authoritative enough to be quoted at length by Charles Darwin in *The Voyage of the Beagle*.[8]

Holman is a great example of a figure from history with real power to change what people expect of the blind today, as well as what the blind can expect of themselves. In an era when the odds were stacked sky-high against disabled people, he had the mettle and emotional resilience to prove prevailing naysayers wrong, and exemplify that no environment, career, or dream is truly inaccessible to the blind. But Holman is also a great example of the problem, because – as has happened to so many others through the ages – toxic, ignorant ways of thinking about blindness caused him to fall between the cracks of history.

A rival adventurer was first to sow seeds of contempt, asking: "Who will then say that Siberia is a wild, inhospitable, or impassable country, when even the blind can traverse it safely?"[9] This critique mutated into the generally accepted idea that blindness rendered any observational work void and valueless.[10] In response to Holman's book on circumnavigating the globe (published in the early 1830s), one critic wrote: "A want of verification… renders the work almost if not entirely useless."[11] Another cruelly asserted that: "Deprivation of sight bears along with it a physical barrier to investigation in foreign lands, which no talent or judgment can surmount."[12]

In the end, Holman – progressively painted as a gimmick and a novelty – fell victim to history's broad scythe of forgetfulness. All his original manuscripts were gradually lost or destroyed after his death, and encyclopaedia entries about The Blind Traveller shrank with each edition printed, until eventually, he slipped off the paper's edge for good. He's not alone: accomplished blind people through the ages have fallen in great numbers out of our textbooks, biographies, and anthologies. This trend was recognised even in Holman's time: when the blind and self-taught James Wilson compiled his *Biography of the Blind* in 1820, he did so "with a view of rescuing my fellow sufferers from the neglect and obscurity in which many of them are involved".[13]

Yet Wilson's words hold as true now as they did 200 years ago. The same harmful views on blindness that let Holman fade into the mists of almost total anonymity are still rampant today, and so we're in danger of repeating history's mistakes. In 2015, more than a third of blind people in the UK reported that they sometimes, frequently, or always experienced negative attitudes from the general public, and nearly half of those of working age said they had been treated unfairly because of their disability in the last 12 months.[14] These incidents of unfair treatment are most often caused by strangers on the street (63%), followed by retail staff and bus drivers. That the main offenders are those characters who populate our everyday lives – whom we encounter casually and frequently – is most indicative of an endemic social problem, rooted in ignorance.

Discriminatory ways of thinking can also lead to violence. The UK has seen alarming increases in the number of disability hate crimes (these numbers surged by 14% in England and Wales between 2018-19), and similarly disturbing trends have been recorded all around the world.[15]

We can only expect people to do better than they are – whether that's patronising, objectifying, underestimating or outright attacking the blind – if we educate them, and show by example why they are wrong to think the way they do.

It's not just that we aren't giving people the knowledge they need to engage with blindness in a healthy, authentic way – we are actively doing the opposite, and disseminating dangerous misinformation about sight loss. Misrepresentation in pop culture is so rampant that the general public's understanding is built in large part on fabricated falsehoods, myths about blindness that crop up on our TV screens and are subsequently internalised and perpetuated. Toxic ways of thinking proliferate precisely because they've been so normalised: we see clichés and stereotypes of the blind so often that we think they're real. I know this, because before I went blind myself, I too accepted these lies as truths without question.

Pop culture portrayals tend to conform to one of two polarities. First, there's the helpless blind person, totally dependent on others; this can range from forlorn, pitiable wretchedness to comedic ineptitude. At the other end of the spectrum, there is the blind superhuman, where a lack of vision must be compensated for with some other incredible power, whether that's clairvoyance (as in 1973's *Don't Look Now*) or the ability to lie detect by hearing heartbeats from metres away (2003's *Daredevil*).

We're all familiar with the tropes associated with these uninformed imaginings of a real community. On-screen blind men creepily sniff women's necks (1992's *Scent of a Woman* or *Daredevil* again). Sighted characters embark on the classic con or comic foil of pretending to be blind for sympathy, money, or laughs (the American season six of *The Office*, or 2019's *The Heist* and *Happy Death Day 2U*). A lack of vision somehow translates into a character being unbelievably stupid and displaying a complete unawareness of what they are doing – and this can involve someone else's sexual gratification (*Ali G Indahouse* (2002), or 1993's *Robin Hood: Men In Tights*).

Blindness in pop culture is also invariably being faked (*Trading Places* (1973) or 2012's *Red Lights*), or can magically be cured to restore the protagonist to able-bodied normality (2013's *Anchorman 2: The Legend Continues*). Blind characters flail across our TV screens in a constant state of reminding audiences of their only personality trait: blindness (whether that's by stating it over and over, careening wildly into obstacles, or engaging in excessive face touching).

What's more, in each of these examples and so many more, all these blind characters are depicted by sighted actors. The likes of Val Kilmer, Audrey Hepburn, Denzel Washington, Ralph Fiennes, Rebel Wilson, Ben Affleck, and Al Pacino have all graced our screens playing largely uninformed, lazy caricatures of the blind, in cultural products scripted, directed, and produced by other sighted people. So when inevitable mistakes are made, experiences assumed, and realities altered, no one involved is equipped to make corrections.

It matters when these people get it wrong – the majority of their audience, too, isn't informed enough to identify misrepresentation when they see it. And so the cycle continues. When these images and narratives are all the general public has for reference, it's no wonder real-life blind people suffer micro-aggressions on the street, discrimination and low expectations at work and in schools, and poor mental health. Pop culture has trained us all to think of blindness as either totally tragic or completely comedic.

For Liverpool-based blind writer and director Mandy Redvers-Rowe, one cultural product stands out in particular for its offensive depiction of the blind experience: *Crystal Clear*, an 80-minute play devised by director Phil Young and the piece's three actors, and first performed in a ramshackle North London pub in 1982. By spring the following year it had graduated onto the glitz and glamour of a West End stage, and was "the most rapturously received event of the season", according to *New York Times* theatre critic Benedict Nightingale.[16]

A love triangle at its core, the play tells the story of diabetic Richard (who loses his sight during the play), his partner Jane, and love interest Thomasina (who is blind throughout). In his review, Nightingale gushes about the lengths went to by the sighted cast, as they prepared to – publicly and for profit – engage with a real-life disability: "To help stimulate their imaginations," he writes, "they learned to walk the streets, go shopping, or simply move about their own homes with their eyes completely covered."[17] The characters they subsequently devised grapple with "helplessness and self-disgust", the "dread of being trapped forever in a windowless ghetto", and a desire for children, which is painted as impossible for someone without sight to fulfil.[18]

"I felt so defeated," Mandy tells me. She saw the play in her twenties, when it first came out. "I thought, how dare you imagine my life and get it so wrong. And then take it on a national tour, and continue these terrible, terrible images of us – awful images of blind and visually impaired people who are dependent and helpless. That is not who we are. In our fight for the public and the mainstream to see us as positive and exciting and interesting, there is a whole group of people making money – let's be clear about this – with all this false information about us."

That this play was so well-received speaks volumes about the ignorance of its original audience. One critic proclaimed it "undoubtedly the most moving play in London, and one of the most intelligent", and another professed his heart torn out "in anguished sympathy".[19] Yet another blind Victorian's words ring painfully true here – an unnamed intellectual who said: "I assure you it is not blindness, but its consequences, which we feel most painfully, and those consequences are often laid on us most heavily by the people who are loudest in their expressions of pity."[20] And to those who might argue that the play – and the words of its critics – are products of their time, *Crystal Clear* was revived in the summer of 2019 to further positive reviews.[21]

We need to recognise the ways in which misrepresentation is damaging to real-life communities. F Scott Fitzgerald wrote that part of the beauty of literature was that: "You discover that your longings are universal longings, that you're not lonely and isolated from anyone. You belong."[22] For decades pop culture has been telling blind people the exact opposite, and so it's hardly surprising that the community struggles with their mental health.

If we recognise the problems at play, we can begin fixing them. We can champion the blind people who want to participate in the creation and distribution of narratives concerning their disability. We can recognise both that they can contribute nuanced, true-to-life depictions of their experiences to the pop culture landscape – and that these are much needed. For Mandy, this goal fundamentally underpins her work. "I have a drive in me, fuelled by a sense that people need to understand that my experience as a blind person is not the one you think it is," she explains. "That's what I'm driven by. I do not like to be patronised. I do not want the world to pity me. I want the world to see how amazing my life is, and other disabled people's lives."

Early in her career, Mandy used comedy as a vehicle ("Everyone sees disability as sad and dismal. So we're going to challenge that by being funny, and silly, and by having a lot of fun with life"). One skit, which formed part of an alphabetical mini-series by disabled comedy trio No Excuses and broadcast on BBC2 in the 1990s, sought to highlight the problematic nature of *Crystal Clear*. In the skit (entitled *O is for Oscars*), Mandy depicts fictional actor Angelina Brooks, winning a Golden Globe for playing a woman who loses her sight in a film called *Clear as Mud*. Angelina explains how she got into character: "I put on a blindfold, borrowed my neighbour's poodle, and felt everything. And I also felt it was important to suffer, because I think that blind people do. Don't you?"

Mandy has since turned her hand to writing drama for television, stage, and radio to counterbalance historic misrepresentation. In 2019, her radio play *Blind School* – featuring a cast of blind voice actors – was broadcast on BBC Radio 4, telling the story of new student Nina, who joins a school for the blind while experiencing progressive sight loss. Her most recent TV drama, *Second Sight* (broadcast on BBC1 in early 2020), aimed to show audiences that regaining one's ability to see is "not this fairy tale that people think it's going to be", with a story "challenging enough to make people rethink their attitudes to blindness and to sight gain". We can all participate in destabilising the buildup of insidious misinformation by promoting the work of blind writers like Mandy, as they take back control of narratives about their disability.

We can also work harder to reestablish in our collective memories the great numbers of brilliant blind people still languishing in the deep dark corners of history's hard drive. These examples from the past have so much power to change perceptions of the blind, and it's not too late to brush off the dust and add them to our curricula and our general knowledge banks. One person striving to help the public do just that is Michele Mele, a blind research fellow in mathematics at the University of Sannio in southern Italy. When the coronavirus pandemic hit in March 2020, Michele began compiling a book about blind scientists – entitled *The Universe Between the Fingers* (published as *L'Universo tra le Dita* in January 2021) – to combat prejudice rooted in ignorance.

His book catalogues such figures as Nicholas Saunderson (1682-1739), blinded by smallpox aged one, who went on to occupy one of the most prestigious academic positions in Europe: Lucasian Professor of Mathematics at the University of Cambridge. This post has also been held by the likes of Isaac Newton, Charles Babbage, and Stephen Hawking.[23] Saunderson did not come from money and was almost entirely self-taught. He built his own abacus-like device (called a "palpable arithmetic") using a ridged wooden board, pins, and thread, allowing him to master complex mathematical and geometric ideas independently. He was a gifted and dedicated teacher: one student who attended his lectures in the 1710s described him as someone "who did not have the use of his eyes, but taught others to use theirs".[24]

Another historical figure populating Michele's pages is John Metcalf (1717-1810), known affectionately as Blind Jack, one of the forefathers of modern civil engin-eering.[25] Blind from the age of six, Metcalf designed and helped construct around 180 miles of road in the North of England (much of which still survives), and was one of the first professionals of this kind in the country.[26] He also pioneered a way for roads to span marshland, using rafts made of the thorny evergreen gorse and springy purple heather that stipple so much of his local landscape with colour to this day.

More well-known is the Swiss mathematician Leonhard Euler (1707-1783). Euler exhibited extraordinary and unparalleled prolificacy over his career – he made significant contributions to a mind-bogglingly diverse array of fields, including cartography, magnetism, shipbuilding, hydraulics, music, and our understanding of the moon; he also developed much of the mathematical notation so familiar today (for example, $f(x)$ for function and π for pi).[27] When his eyesight began to deteriorate in middle age, his reaction was: "Now I will have fewer distractions." His productivity rose to even more dizzying heights. By the end of his career, he had written close to 900 books – half of them while almost completely blind and around a third while partially sighted. After his death, publishing his previously unpublished work took the St Petersburg Academy nearly half a century. He is the most prolific mathematician of all time.

Michele explains the logic of why we need to remember these figures, and that they were blind. "People don't want to have prejudice; it's just that the human mind is made that way. You have to just fight it, and perseverance and by example are the best ways. You have to lead by example, and at the same time you have to show that someone has already done it. We all stand on the shoulders of giants – so it's exactly the same to show that if a blind person managed to be one of the greatest mathematicians of his time, why can't a blind person now?

"It's like when you say a mathematical assertion, a proposition, and then you find a counterexample – something that proves your thesis wrong – and that means it's not a proposition but a false statement, and you have to formulate it again. If we do that, I think people will understand slowly. It's not a drastic solution, and it will take decades. But if we manage to put good routines in place, in schools and in the media, and start pointing out the problems when people are young, it becomes a routine, something that they do unconsciously. The first time, they'll think about it – the second time, they'll think about it – but the third time, it will come more naturally, and they will just think it's normal."

Putting in the work Michele is talking about will benefit everyone, because we all lose when we diminish the value of a whole community and waste the opportunity to harness a capable workforce with largely untapped social, cultural, and economic utility. In 2020, the employment rate for the blind in the UK was only 27%, compared to 76% for the general population and 51% for the disabled population when excluding sight loss.[28] The indirect cost of blindness (factoring in productivity loss through lower employment and associated reductions in wellbeing), has been estimated to be around £24bn a year.[2] That's more than £65m a day. So if we can break down vicious cycles of ignorance and prejudice, and instead reconfigure new, virtuous cycles of thought and behaviour, we will all reap the benefits.

Although there are big, long-term goals in play here, small changes are all that's required to get a domino effect started. Empowering just one person who might otherwise not have felt able to accomplish anything may seem like an intimate, microcosmic act without much impact – but the effects of doing so can ripple out exponentially. Michele is keen to reinforce this point: "When the environment gives blind and partially sighted people the chance to shine, it gives the environment itself the possibility to improve, and to other people, new chances." One great example of this ripple effect is the story of Anne Sullivan (1866 – 1936), who demonstrates that changing one life is a worthwhile act that gets passed on.

Blind from the age of five, Sullivan grew up in an infamously deplorable Massachusetts almshouse after her mother died and her father abandoned the family.[30] When local officials finally conducted an investigation into the horrific conditions at the almshouse, she pleaded with them to send her to school. Her heartfelt appeal worked, and after graduating from the Perkins School for the Blind, Sullivan taught a tempestuous, deafblind seven-year-old to read, write, and express herself. Her student grew up to be the hugely influential author and activist Helen Keller (1880-1968), who would later describe the day she met her teacher and lifelong companion – March 3rd, 1887 – as "my soul's birthday".[31] Sullivan had to fight tooth and nail for an education and a chance to prove herself, and when she got it, she transformed the life of another into something extraordinary: a life that touched and improved countless others.

Enacting these virtuous cycles may take time – but we know that it can be done, and that once they are in place, they really can make a difference. Amadou has seen the transformative power of increased visibility in action over his lifetime. He explains that growing up in Mali in the 1960s, people's perceptions of the blind were limited by the fact that they most often saw them begging on the streets, as no structures existed to give the blind access to work or training. "It was like that everywhere," Amadou said. "And when people had children and they were blind, often they would hide them in the house."

Then, in 1973, the Institute for Young Blind People – l'Institut des Jeunes Aveugles (IJA) – was established in Bamako, the country's capital, and became ground zero for far-reaching societal shifts. "The IJA changed mentalities – not just those of the general public, but of the blind as well," said Amadou. "It tried to show people that the blind can do something with their lives, and promoted many activities both to bring blind people closer to the community and to make the community understand our reality. It really changed social conditions for the blind."

The IJA was so successful that in 2012, roughly half of the 367-strong student body were not even blind – they had simply selected the institute for its academic excellence.[32] While Amadou & Mariam are certainly the school's most famous exports (the Grammy nominees have played the main stage at Glastonbury, and supported Coldplay, Blur, and U2 on tour), other graduates have gone on to the likes of prestigious civil service roles – a far cry from the beggaring that blindness might have destined them for fifty years earlier.

The IJA was also where – one March morning in 1975 – new student Amadou was touring classrooms and met a girl whose voice he knew from a well-known song of the time. Everyone in the room began to sing, and Amadou and Mariam Doumbia's voices rang out together for the first time. Nearly half a century on, these grandparents are still making music alongside one another, their upbeat, multilingual vocals overlapping over the sound of Amadou dexterously strumming or shredding his golden guitar. For this is the true power of visibility – seeing one another allows us to connect, and forge intimate, emotional bonds that can truly transform our lives.

We all deserve access to these bonds, and those who have experienced forming them can testify to their positive emotional impact. For Michele, it was a young Nicholas Saunderson, learning to read and perform calculations with his father, that had the most profound effect. "The first time I read his story, I was so close to crying, because his father sounds very similar to my mother [a secondary school maths and physics teacher], who is the most influential person in my life." For Amadou, it was Ray Charles with whom he felt a deep, empathetic bond: not only did both men have sight loss and musical careers in common, but they lost younger brothers in bathing accidents as children. On this, Amadou has written: "When I heard that Ray Charles had had the same unhappy experience, I smiled. I understood that hardship, blindness, that death of a loved one, had shown us both the way through life."[33]

For me, it was James Holman, who – in some twist of fate – was buried in Highgate Cemetery, just ten minutes from where I grew up. This historic North London graveyard is no stranger to celebrity: there are people lying beneath the loam whose names everybody knows. Karl Marx, Christina Rossetti, Douglas Adams, and George Eliot are all here. There's scenery that played across the silver screen as the set of various 1970s horror movies, and gorgeous, theatrical structures that tell stories of the Victorian fascination with Ancient Egypt,

Greece, and Rome, as well as their flair for the gothic. Even in the safety of a bright, spring afternoon, it's easy to imagine this same landscape dripping with macabre drama in the dark.

But I don't care. It's not the famous or gruesome that's brought me here: I've come specifically to pay tribute to the forgotten. Holman's grave, when I find it, is unremarkable, set beside a wide, clean stretch of new asphalt, in which particles of ground glass sparkle underfoot. Twisting, pale green shapes left by the stripping away of ivy coil across the headstone like florets of bleached coral. There are no angels or obelisks here, and no mausoleum with a vaulted golden ceiling. There's just a skip full of rubbish, and a heap of cement sacks that resemble the bodies of sleeping animals. But to me, the space around Holman's headstone is the most beautiful place in the world.

Chapter 2:
On accessibility

When I was eight, a childhood friend told me that there was a secret button underneath the control boxes at pedestrian crossings, and that if I spun it between my fingers, the green man would appear straight away. I had been wondering what those small metal stalactites were: they seemed to come to life in such mysterious, arbitrary ways, and no one had ever explained their true use to me. But even thinking that they had the power to speed up a journey, I avoided them. In winter, they were so cold to the touch that it burned – and reaching for them led all too often to recoiling with a shudder as my skin brushed gauzy spiderwebs or chewing gum, sometimes still wet with a stranger's saliva.

In reality, these cones spin not on demand, but when

the green man is already illuminated, signalling to blind people that it's safe to cross the road. Now that I use these whenever I go out, I don't have the luxury of choosing not to fish in grimy shadows, or grip freezing metal for minutes at a time. Gloves aren't an option, because I can't always feel the cones spin through fabric – especially as some are so sluggish it takes time to confirm they really are turning. But worse than all of that is when the cones are not there at all. Then, I must make a choice sighted people never have to, even though they cross roads every day. I can be safe, or I can be independent: the city does not allow me to be both simultaneously.

According to a 2014 survey by the RNIB, 55% of blind people said their local roads were unsafe; 74% said there was a need for more pedestrian crossings in their area, and 67% had to make longer, more inconvenient journeys just to hit accessible crossings on their route.[1] The RNIB also found that only about half of local councils could provide any information about the accessibility of the crossings they were in charge of managing.[2] When I once tried to report a non-functioning cone, the person I spoke to had no idea what I was talking about, and I realised I didn't even know the name of the device myself. My friend had been right about one thing: the feature truly was a secret.

Crossing the road is just the beginning. As soon as I step out the door, I'm hounded by problems of access which conspire to make me feel frustrated, angry, or miserable – and always unwelcome. On the tube, visual-only cues signal the direction an escalator is travelling, whether an oyster gate is an exit or entrance, and how to change from one line to another. Sometimes, a train will play muffled or crackly announcements through long-broken speakers; on other occasions, activating these audio tracks is forgotten altogether. In each instance, the burden is on me to plug the gaps I find, and so a hundred times over on even the most mundane trip, I'm forced to ask myself: should I compromise my autonomy here, and ask for help? My only other option is to battle it out against the most authoritative of opponents: an entrenched system that seems to support almost everyone except me. Nothing is effortless. Life becomes like a video game I just can't quit, even though I'm tired of fighting.

The obstacles that I, and countless other blind people, face every day are not just issues of design, but of attitude. The way we think about accessibility – the practice of making something usable and useful for as many people as possible – is extremely problematic, and the rotating cones at pedestrian crossings are an excellent example. Firstly, we haven't even been given the language to talk about them, reflecting the way that blind experiences are treated like shameful secrets that society must keep hidden. These life-saving devices may be both critical and ordinary to the blind – but for everyone else, they are so mysterious that they're fodder for urban myths that adults aren't informed enough to dispel.

The cones also don't form part of the design of crossing control boxes: they are made by a separate company, and must be retro-fitted.[3] This reflects the way that accessibility is almost always an afterthought, not an intrinsic part of something's design or conception. It's perceived as a tick-box exercise to meet baseline legal requirements, something that must be bolted on after the fact to serve a tiny minority of users, who are all too often considered negligible in number or worth. We don't think it can be creative or beautiful, and companies designing products or environments often don't see any financial incentive to invest in it. As a result, it is critically undeveloped and undervalued in almost every sphere.

Accessibility has a serious image problem – and we need to fix it.

Current attitudes surrounding accessibility are cruel, and punish the blind for something that is part of who they are. It doesn't take much imagination to comprehend the emotional toll of endlessly being at war with the world around you because of something you cannot change. One woman, Joyce, who was interviewed by the RNIB when they conducted research into blind people's movements around their local areas in 2015, said that even though inaccessible conditions prevailed, she made herself keep on travelling "because if I stopped going out

I'd never go out again".[4] But the mental health implications exist in every scenario – for the blind people forced to stay home and lead lonely, isolated lives, and for those who go out and encounter exclusive and discriminatory systems.

This, in turn, sparks a sinister ripple effect. Inaccessible environments hinder the blind community's participation in work and leisure pursuits outside the home, which in turn means lower visibility for the community, amplifying existing ignorance surrounding blindness. This is not just the case in the UK. One 2020 study conducted in Seoul tracking the travel patterns of blind people using mobile phone data found that accessible pedestrian infrastructure was "the most critical factor" affecting whether, and how often, blind people travelled around built environments.[5] We wonder why the blind live so much in the shadows – it's because we've made the light unsafe and unwelcoming.

We need to recognise the way in which our attitude towards accessibility renders us complicit in these self-fulfilling cycles. We are active players: it was reported in 2019 that 76% of guide dog owners had been illegally refused entry to businesses and services, like taxis, cafes, hotels, pubs, and shops, by uninformed proprietors.[6] Unsurprisingly, 70% said this had a negative emotional impact. We must be made aware of the fact that not granting someone access to a place or experience that someone with sight can enter without even thinking does real, palpable harm.

When Dr. Mona Minkara, a blind computational chemist and Assistant Professor of Bioengineering at Northeastern University in Massachusetts, embarked on a project exploring accessibility in five cities around the globe, she found London the least accessible – and people's attitudes were a big part of the problem. "To me, it was the most emotionally exhausting city," she said. "From an infrastructure perspective, Johannesburg was less accessible, but London was the least accessible from an emotional health perspective. I like London, and there are a lot of great Londoners, but there's a lot of: 'Where's your caretaker?' That question, innately, is: 'Where's the person in charge of dealing with you, because I don't want to.' That's how it came off."

Mona's project (which won the 2019 Holman Prize, named for James Holman, receiving funding from the San Francisco Lighthouse for the Blind and Visually Impaired) centred around creating a short series on YouTube called "Planes, Trains, and Canes", documenting her explorations of London, Singapore, Tokyo, Istanbul, and Johannesburg.[7] Her London footage is harrowing to watch in places. People ignore her on the street when she asks for help, and address her video-grapher (who follows at a distance without intervening) instead of her, even after being told why doing so is inappropriate. In a tube station, a Transport for London employee tells her she must accept assistance if she's travelling alone. When Mona explains that the point of her trip is to explore spontaneously and independently, he tells her she doesn't have a choice: she's a liability.

"[That incident] really hit on the point of autonomy for people with disabilities, because there's this innate sense that when you have a disability, you are a burden. [In London,] the culture is systematically built so that you are discouraged from doing things, and so I'm an oddity for being a blind person on my own on the tube. And this system is so deeply embedded that people literally forgot to connect on a human level. I'm not asking for the world here! But it was like a battle, just to be left alone as a human being."

Treating the blind – and disabled people more broadly – as problem people, as opposed to acknowledging and fixing the obstacles they face, is to everyone's detriment, not least because it's extremely short-sighted. On the most basic level, the human body is changeable: absolutely anybody can fall out of the able-bodied majority, at any time. So while problems of inaccessibility might not affect you now, they almost certainly will at some point over your lifetime. The World Health Organisation currently estimates more than 1 billion people live with a disability worldwide (around 15% of the global population), and this number is on the rise.[8] What's more, they note that almost everybody will, at some point or other, experience a disability, either permanent or temporary. It's "part of being human".[9]

We also hold back the progress of the whole human race when we disregard accessibility, because we are excluding large groups of people from pursuing careers in a wide variety of sectors to which they could be making valuable contributions. We have already learned about how blind people are systematically undervalued and underestimated, leading to a self-fulfilling prophecy of low expectations and low employment rates. Poor accessibility plays a key role in this vicious cycle. It can be a significant obstacle in career development, whereby blind professionals are forced to solve problems their sighted colleagues won't ever encounter. But it can also deter young people from pursuing certain pathways in the first place, acting as a needless roadblock and ensuring we waste the opportunity to harness all that potential.

Dr. Nicolas Bonne is a blind astronomer at the University of Portsmouth, specialising in galaxy evolution and formation, who also works in a public engagement role. But it was no easy road to get there, and in his line of work he sees others embarking on much the same journey, decades after him. "Alternative ways of learning about astronomy, for somebody who's less visual, didn't really exist when I was little," Nic said (he fell in love with space when he was five). "And there haven't been many steps forward in terms of making astronomy too much more accessible since.

"So there are young people [with vision impairments] at the point where they're thinking science is cool, but there are enough people in their lives saying: 'No, you shouldn't do that, it's going to be too difficult.' The influence of the people around us can be really strong, especially if somebody says you shouldn't do something because you'll find it too hard. That can become a reality for you really, really quickly."

This exclusion isn't just about numbers, whereby the disabled community make up a large swathe of the global population who aren't getting a fair chance to actualise their potential. This is about the value of perspectives that differ from the able-bodied norm. Blindness invites those it touches not only to see, but to think, differently: they must constantly engage in creative problem solving as they navigate a world built around a tool they lack. So when we create problems of access, we are actively excluding the very viewpoints that have the most power to push us to innovate and advance.

Welcoming a diverse spectrum of viewpoints into the scientific community can enact great good. Think of the seismic changes made by Dr. Temple Grandin, the scientist, inventor, and animal behaviourist with autism, who used her detail-oriented "thinking in pictures" to revolutionise livestock handling practices, designing humane, cruelty-free systems still in use to this day.[10] Grandin is just one example of how diversity in science engenders the kind of innovation that is the bedrock of human progress: identifying problems, and designing creative solutions, in a way that advances us all as societies, and as moral and intellectual beings.

For Mona, there was a lightbulb moment where she realised her blindness could actually be an asset in her field. While completing her Chemistry PhD in Florida, Mona was approached by Professor J. Ilja Siepmann at the University of Minnesota. "He basically said: 'Come, you have a job with me.' I remember I had a meeting with him and it turned into more like me interviewing him, as opposed to him interviewing me. That's how deeply I had internalised the idea that my blindness was something that I needed to overcome, that I needed to run a little bit harder to keep up with my peers, because I was lacking this tool."

Her interview with Siepmann changed all that. "I asked him: 'Do you know that I work a little slower? Do you know that I'm blind?' And he said: '*Because* you are blind, I can recognise that you will be able to solve problems that nobody else can solve, because you have to think differently. We need to propagate that kind of thinking in the scientific community.' And I thought, wow. It just hit me."

Siepmann is absolutely right – we can all harness this resource by encouraging the participation of the blind in science and innovation spheres, rather than deterring and hindering them. But another way we can harness that imaginative strength is by working to make our world more accessible, because the very practice of developing accessibility for the blind calls for us to find ways of doing things without using our eyes. We already know from history that this innovation catalyst can do great things. Ever used a flatbed scanner, or read any of the 60,000 classic works of literature digitised and made available for free online by Project Gutenberg?[11] Ever used real-time translation software, like Google Translate, where you can input your text and immediately have it converted to another language, which your computer can show you how to pronounce? All of these capabilities – and many more, from automatic number plate recognition to searchable PDFs – come from one singular piece of technology and its development: OCR (optical character recognition), the process by which written text is converted into data. Your computer not only recognises this data, but – crucially – knows what to do with it next.

Although its mechanical lineage dates back to pre-WWI, OCR was completely revolutionised in the last quarter of the 20th century by Kurzweil Computer Products, Inc.[12] The company's founder, Ray Kurzweil, wanted to harness the potential of OCR to create a machine that would allow books to be read aloud to the blind by a computer, and in working to make this happen, he also invented the flatbed scanner and a sophisticated text-to-speech synthesiser.[13] Once the digital age had truly dawned, the applications for OCR technology became virtually endless. Today, all of these byproducts of Kurzweil's drive to make written text accessible to the blind impact the lives of billions of humans across the planet.

There are other advantages to being pushed out of the comfort zone of sight, and exploring how our other senses can be better put to use – because relying on our primary sense alone is not always good for us. Our dependence on visual perception means we can fall victim to the "streetlight effect", a kind of observational bias often explained in the form of a joke. Imagine that late one night, a patrolling police officer finds a drunk man, on his hands and knees, scouring the ground beneath a streetlight for something he's lost. She kneels down to help him look. Together they search every inch of the illuminated asphalt, until she asks him: "Are you sure this is where you dropped it?" The man replies: "No; I dropped it in the park, but this is where the light is."

Our instinct to consume data with our eyes can make us blinkered, biased, or act counterintuitively. Visual bias is a real, tangible phenomenon, and can reveal itself in small, seemingly insignificant ways you likely aren't aware of (cultural background affects depth perception: depending on whether you read languages from left to right or vice versa impacts your ability to judge if something is concave or convex).[14] But it can also be dangerous and insidious; one 2019 study by Cornell University showed that white decision makers visually perceive Black faces as less human during times of economic scarcity, increasing incidences of discrimination.[15]

It's important to be aware of our historic reliance on our eyes, and challenge it, because leaving things as they are creates a cycle of affirmation, devaluing the very many other ways of gathering and understanding data. "Innately, we've been raised and taught that science is visual, observation is visual," Mona tells me. "In reality, there are many different ways to observe, many different ways to do science. But human beings have really validated sight as affirming observation over other methods."

These other methods are well worth exploring. Nic has been developing tools that can make the study of astronomy more inclusive by incorporating the sense of touch, and which can educate and inspire everyone, not just the blind students for whom they will be critical. His Tactile Universe Project uses 3D-printed models of different types of galaxy, to tell stories of how these star systems form and change over time. By running their fingers over the models, users can physically feel how the light changes, with brighter parts raised higher off the base, and the darkest lying flush against it.[16]"If these resources can get to a class with one kid with a vision impairment, and everybody else has perfectly good vision, everyone in that classroom is going to enjoy the session and get something out of it. The kids may actually start talking to each other a little bit more than they otherwise would."

Nic is not alone in fighting to prove that there are other, equally valid ways to explore the world beyond our atmosphere besides visual observation. After the onset of aggressively degenerative sight loss, astrophysicist Dr. Wanda Díaz-Merced felt "excommunicated" from the scientific community – written off as someone who could not contribute productively to her field.[17] But she didn't give up. After completing her physics degree, she interned with Robert Candey at NASA Goddard Spaceflight Centre in Maryland, and together with her mentor, pioneered a way to translate astrophysical data into sound.[18] To put her sonification software to the test, she asked experienced (sighted) scientists at the Centre for Astrophysics in Massachusetts to identify the presence of a black hole from among several simulated datasets, presented as visual only, sound only, and visual and sound modalities combined. The results? Sonifying the data improved subjects' ability to successfully diagnose black hole indicators.

Sonification, clearly, could benefit the field as a whole, not just the blind scientists for whom it was critical. For this very reason, Díaz-Merced was disheartened by the results of her experiment. If analysing data in sound form could help everyone alongside supporting the inclusion of the blind, why had it been unavailable until she herself had been driven to create a way to do it? On this, Díaz-Merced has said: "I felt really disappointed at that moment, because people like me had been completely left out of the field for no reason."[19]

The problem is one of mindset: we're set in our ways. We've affirmed vision, our most comfortable and convenient sense, as the ultimate observational tool to such an extent that we are wasting the potential of using the others. Speaking about what Díaz-Merced's work with sonification means for the scientific community, Nic said: "For a lot of astronomers, it really represents a shift from the very traditional way of doing science. Doing it [in a non-visual way] is very different. It's very new. It's taking a lot of work from those who want to actually turn people around and show them that, yes, this is really viable, this is a way that we can do things."

This is despite decades of knowing how valuable a contribution using our other senses can make to the field. In 1931, radio engineer Karl Jansky (1905-1950) picked up a hissing static sound, the origin of which he couldn't identify.[20] He finally determined that it was coming from the constellation of Sagittarius, which points to the supermassive black hole at the heart of the Milky Way. Jansky had become the first person in the world to detect extra-terrestrial radio waves, an observation which led to the emergence of the field of radio astronomy – and he did it by listening.

Our sense of hearing is an excellent example of a power we could be putting to better, more focused use than we currently are. Sound consultant Julian Treasure, delivering a 2009 TED talk on how sound affects us, explains that the way we engage with aural information is "largely unconscious": sound is something that wafts constantly and accidentally around us, seeming not to have much utility, direction, or purpose.[21] But Treasure is keen to convey that we could be having a much richer, more fulfilling relationship with what we hear, and this can improve every aspect of our lives.

Treasure lays out the four key ways that sound is impacting us all the time. First, there's the physiological impact (examples might include how loud, sudden noises can affect hormone secretions, raise our heart rate, and affect breathing – or how surf is soothing because it has roughly the same number of cycles per minute as a sleeping human's breath). Second, the psychological (the way music can make us feel emotions, or how birdsong reassures us and improves productivity, because of the link forged in primeval times between birds singing and safety). The third way is cognitive (we find it hard to understand messy, overlapping sounds, like two people talking at once), and the fourth is behavioural (we move away from unpleasant sounds; if we can't, it's extremely detrimental to our health).

Treasure, moreover, presents some compelling statistics to show how sound is not being properly utilised – and why it should be. Commercial businesses could be increasing the impact of their messages by over 1100% if they were to use sound in a congruent, appropriate way alongside visual communication. Using sound badly, however, reduces a message's impact by 86%. Oblivious retail stores are driving away up to 30% of business simply by bombarding customers with unpleasant sound, affecting consumer patterns of behaviour. People are 33% as productive when working in a noisy open-plan office – but play birdsong to employees and productivity triples.

The very challenge of designing accessibility measures for those who cannot see naturally calls our attention to how sound might be employed more consciously. Much of the assistive technology used by blind people every day relies on translating visual cues into audio, from screen readers (either a handheld device or software which reads aloud any text on screen), audio description (audible narration of what sighted audiences can see in a film or TV show) or kitchen gadgets, like talking scales or clip-on liquid level indicators, which beep when their user is close to filling their cup.

But the point is that a more conscious use of sensory information other than visual need not be limited to assisting the blind community – both developing it in a creative way, and putting it to use in our environments, can help many more people have a more fulfilling relationship with sound. Think about how useful mainstream technologies like Siri, Google Assistant, and Alexa are; think about being able to have navigation guidance read aloud to you while you drive. And it's not just about innovations that make our lives more streamlined and efficient – it's about culture and leisure pursuits too. The podcasting boom (as of March 2021, Apple Podcasts alone host close to 2m podcasts, up 60% from 2018) clearly shows an appetite for imaginative content creation and consumption that is non-visual.[22]

All of these things are accessible to the blind, but helpful and valuable for others, too, the same way that curb cuts (where the pavement slopes down to meet the level of the road) are advantageous for people with luggage or prams, for example, as well as critical for the wheelchair users for whom they were designed. As *Brooklyn Nine Nine*'s Jake Peralta argues: "Stuff can be two things!" Accessibility measures can, and absolutely will, do more than just their critical design purpose.

If any environment exemplifies this, it's Tokyo. When Mona visited the city as part of "Planes, Trains, and Canes", she found a design approach and cultural attitude worlds away from emotionally exhausting London, and it improved the space for all. Not only are there audio signals at pedestrian crossings, but there are two different sounds they make, depending on whether you are crossing the road on a north-south or an east-west axis. Escalators speak to you, announcing whether they are going up or down. Tourism centres, which proliferate all across Japan, carry specific pamphlets catering to a disabled audience, explaining accessible features of transit systems and public spaces. Temporary tactile paving is installed to guide the blind around unpredictable street furniture, like construction work (in a city as choked by construction as London, this basic courtesy of remembering that blind people exist would be most welcome).

But Tokyo's accessibility showstopper is its tube stations. Here, auditory information abounds; the sound of running water marks the toilets, and birdsong, the exits. What's more, each station has its own unique, seven-second melody, which plays to announce a train's arrival and departure. Some of these jingles have cultural relevance: Takadanobaba station, for example, plays the *Astroboy* theme music on its platforms, because it's where the classic manga and anime series is set.[23] But most are original compositions, hand-crafted to suit each neighbourhood by Mukaiya Minoru, combining his love of trains with decades of experience playing keyboards in the jazz fusion band Casiopea.[24]

This practice of using melodies in place of alarms or additional announcements was not specifically designed for the blind – nearly 7m people use the Tokyo metro system every day, and these jingles' purpose is to make the experience as calming and pleasant as possible. But they perfectly demonstrate that accessibility features do not have to be niche, ugly, or bolted on after the fact: rather, they can be integrated seamlessly into design, and be useful for everyone. These seven-second songs streamline and reduce the stress of the daily commute, as well as making navigating the tube easier for those who do not see.

More than that, the jingles show that accessibility can be beautiful and emotional, too – not just functional. Mukaiya's jingles are so popular and beloved that entire blogs have been dedicated to cataloguing them.[25] You can even buy little keychains that play your favourite station's melody, or alarm clocks that play longer tracks of multiple jingles strung together (the Tōzai line melodies between Nakano and Nishifunabashi, for example, form one cohesive song entitled "A Day in the Metro").[26]

"It was phenomenal," Mona said. "There were cane guides everywhere, audio markers everywhere. These things clicked, and they were useful, and it was amazing, and I can't explain how freeing that was. I was just another person in the crowds. And it made me feel like, who needs sight anyway? That is amazing to me. I've never had that experience anywhere else in the world. I was just blown away."

This is the approach we all need to understand and embrace: the idea that it is actually not what is classified as a disability, but rather the world – how it is physically designed and socially organised – that acts as a disabling force in someone's life. This is known as the social model of disability, and is usually considered in contrast to the medical model, which looks at what is physically wrong with a person. Learning about the social model worldview in her twenties, years after losing her sight, was truly transformative for Mandy Redvers-Rowe, the writer and director we met in the previous chapter. "It absolutely blew my mind. And for the first time, helped me make sense of myself.

"Disabled people have always existed. I'm a disabled person; I'm normal. What has happened is that society hasn't acknowledged us and hasn't included us. So what we have to do is change society. This is what equality should be about – you should be allowed to be whoever you are, and if you happen to be a disabled person, then the system should be strong enough to support you, without you having to constantly battle it."

To help propagate this mindset in the UK, she works with an organisation called The DisOrdinary Architecture Project, founded by artist Zoe Partington and architect Jos Boys in 2008, which partners and collaborates with disabled artists, policy makers, students, and design professionals.[27] "[We want people] to see access not as a tick box exercise that you have to do at the end of an architectural project, but actually as a creative driver, as a great way of coming up with new and exciting designs that accommodate a wider public."

Across the Atlantic, others, too, are fighting to change the way people think about accessibility. Sina Bahram, a North Carolina-based accessibility consultant, computer scientist, and entrepreneur, is keen to convey how letting the medical model affect how we include blind people in society is problematic. "For me, the frustration doesn't come from blindness as much as it does from the environment in which that blindness acts as quite a significant obstacle to carrying out whatever thing I wish to do," he explains. "And I'm privileged to have a level of knowledge – I'm a computer scientist, I understand how engineering works, I know what goes into building a building, what goes into some levels of city planning. So I understand rather viscerally how things could be better. And there really is no excuse other than lack of consideration."

Sina founded Prime Access Consulting, or PAC, in 2005 to "support building a more inclusive world", and as a result has endless examples of meaningful projects involving accessibility.[28] The one that best captures what the practice truly centres on is a story he tells me about a young man in Alabama, almost completely paralysed, using four buttons on his wheelchair to slowly drive an iPhone. Sina knew he could do better. He built a device like an old Nokia keypad, with a built-in battery and Bluetooth. "It was less than $1 of plastic, a micro-controller, and a little bit of coding. That's it. And I was just so pissed off that nobody had bothered spending a little bit of time to come up with something at least 10 times better than the system he had. So it's things like that that really motivate me. It's very helpful for one person – it might help a couple hundred other people. But at the end of the day, it's meaningful work that makes an impact in someone's life."

This is the beating heart of why accessibility matters: it's about people. We are human beings, and we all deserve to live in a world that treats us as such. But inaccessibility paints the disabled community as problem people, rather than individuals who want to live their lives the same as everybody else. People who want to explore a new city, without risking their safety or compromising their independence. People who want to ride the train without feeling lost or alone, and without being told they are a liability. Children who look up at a swirling sea of stars, and want to translate that passion and curiosity into a career. People who shouldn't be told, and shown, that the world isn't for them – it's for somebody else.

Ultimately all that's left to do is ask the question that should appeal to the most basic part of us as social and moral beings. What is the price of human dignity? If it is worth anything, then accessibility should be worth everything.

Chapter 3:
On culture

Killing time in central London before meeting friends, I pick my way among the pigeons stippling Trafalgar Square with variegated grey tones and head inside the National Portrait Gallery for a scenic indoor stroll. It's my first time here alone in a long time. Playing over the top of a familiar soundscape, matching the one from memories of past visits, is a fresh soloist: the sweeping sound of my white cane as it passes in even semicircles over the marble floor, like the folding and unfolding of a paper fan.

I ask for an audio guide at the front desk, and am shown how to use it. Each portrait with a recording available has a number printed in small, white digits on the corner of the exhibit's tombstone. Already, it's a flawed system: I can't see the number to enter into the audio guide, and far from every portrait has one. After a chunk of wasted time asking other gallery visitors to hunt down and read aloud these all-too-often nonexistent numbers, I find a bench in an empty room and take a seat. Alone, I try plugging random numbers into the audio guide, some of which end up corresponding to real artworks. A fresh veil of blindness seems to drop down to separate me from everyone and everything around me. I'm surrounded by "the most extensive collection of portraits in the world", and yet I am alternately staring at a dispassionate keypad and closing my eyes to listen to information fragments found by chance.[1]

The NPG has a collection of over 215,000 works, and yet audio guides only provide commentary for around 300 of them, and audio description for an even more paltry 140.[2] This means that as a blind visitor to the gallery, I can access only between 0.06-0.1% of the art housed there. The NPG is far from alone. Across all UK museums and galleries, accessibility measures for the blind only ever facilitate engagement with a small fraction of the exhibits on display, a fraction of the time, with specially-designed tours (sometimes involving permissive handling) available only within small and specific windows. This significantly limits free and spontaneous explorations by visitors with sight loss.

This seems especially unjustifiable when the permanent collections of the UK's metropolitan galleries and museums are free, protected by an almost sacred, untouchable subsidy that creates the illusion that art is accessible to everyone, without discriminating. The fact is that in reality, the ability to walk into one of these spaces and freely explore any and all the exhibits as the master of your own time, pleasure, and cultural education is a privilege, and one that is not afforded to everyone in equal measure.

It is not just in the realm of fine art that unequal access abounds. Theatre performances that do feature live audio description are few and far between, and almost always matinees.[3] The UK's biggest braille library, hosted by the RNIB, boasts a collection of over 22,000 titles for adults and children – when more than eight times that number of new titles were published in the UK in 2011 alone.[4] The RNIB's collection also pales in comparison to that of the British Library, which – if you were to view only five items per day – would take you more than 90,000 years to explore in its entirety.[5] The RNIB's would take only 12.

It matters that art, which touts itself as open and accessible to all, is not. The arts matter. They are not luxuries, beautiful add-ons or extravagant commodities. They have social utility, bonding us to each other and our world; they have the capacity to make us feel, process, and express every emotion in the spectrum, and they are a fundamental part of being human. If we examine more closely why art itself is important, we can better under-stand why access to it matters so much and to so many.

So let's start at the beginning.

Around 44,000 years ago, the mottled walls of the Cave of Fingers in Indonesia became host to the ultimate demonstration of higher order consciousness: figurative painting.[6] Inscribed on these dark, wet land-scapes, sculpted by water over millennia and studded with speleothems, are figures that are half-man and half-creature, animals that are now extinct, and the handprints of our distant ancestors, stencilled onto the rock using purplish ochre powder. Even with tens of thousands of years separating us from them, we have something in common with these prehistoric icono-graphers: humanity and, inherent within that, the ability to engage with art.

This ability is not limited to the visual arts alone. Bird bone and mammoth ivory flutes from a cave in southern Germany have been shown using carbon dating to be between 42,000 and 43,000 years old.[7] Some researchers have even theorised that music, which would have helped early homo sapiens maintain larger and more strongly bonded social groups, gave our species the edge over the Neanderthals – pushing our competitors towards their inevitable extinction.[8] And while writing came much later in human history, we know that story-telling is ancient, permeating every world culture in a multitude of forms, from myths and fables to songs and epic poems, going back millennia.

This chain linking us to distant prehistory is far from rusted. Modern culture draws on this rich aesthetic and thematic network of ideas all the time. Hollywood endlessly recycles the plot of the world's oldest piece of written literature, the Epic of Gilgamesh, which dates back to c. 2150-1400 BCE (the cinema trope of the hero's quest and the nemesis-turned-ally are, literally, the oldest tricks in the book). Another example might be the plethora of 20th century artists who appropriated the enduring visual languages of colonised and indigenous peoples to evolve modern art. Cubism – which seemed so fresh and revolutionary – was in very large part sparked by a visit Pablo Picasso made to the Trocadero Museum of Ethnography in Paris, to see its collection of African masks.[9]

Art also affects much more than just its own descendant forms – it has shaped the way our societies work and defined our entire moral universe. Religious texts, for example – containing poems, songs, and parables – underpin so many of the physical and psychological mechanisms still governing our lives today. Homer's *Iliad* and *Odyssey* similarly laid out the ethics of Ancient Greek society, offering us precious and authentic glimpses into how those people thought and felt. We still use art today to symbolise our morality and humanity. It can represent the values to which we aspire – the way that a replica tapestry of Picasso's visceral and overtly anti-war work *Guernica* hung in the United Nations headquarters from 1984 until 2021.[10] And it can articulate when we fail, too, the way that the pacifist painting was covered by a curtain when the US was on the brink of invading Iraq.[11]

Art also acts as an age-old social barometer for changes in these ethics and value systems over time. Think of the riot that broke out at the premiere of Igor Stravinsky's ballet *The Rite of Spring* in Paris, 1913, or the obscenity trial surrounding D H Lawrence's novel *Lady Chatterley's Lover* in England in 1960.[12] Art has real power to push societies forward, challenging us to interrogate how and why we think and feel about all manner of things. And perhaps most powerfully of all, art can communicate these questions and provocations in a way that transcends spatial, temporal, and linguistic boundaries.

Ultimately, art is something only we human beings can do, and only we can appreciate it. To create it requires emotional, imaginative, and symbolic power; to keep and protect it calls for a complex awareness of the past and the future, something that is unique to us. So where there is a lack of access to arts and culture working against a specific community, we deprive its members of their essential humanity – the chain that links us all to where we've come from and where we can go next. If art is something unique to human beings, then exclusivity and inaccessibility within it is unacceptably dehumanising.

Yet we perpetuate barriers and attitudes that allow such inaccessibility to proliferate. At best, this is the loss of a hobby, a passion or a distraction; at worst, this constitutes depriving the blind of a core emotional and educational experience shared by the entire human race. For some, it's a professional resource and part of their livelihood, too. "For the last 10 years I've got so little out of going to galleries that I don't go any longer," said Keith Salmon, a Scotland-based painter of semi-abstract landscapes. "Isn't that shocking? It shocked me when I thought how few exhibitions I go to."

The inaccessibility of the museum space seems almost farcical when Keith's own paintings depict landscapes that are truly challenging to navigate. Over the last few decades, he's spent hundreds of days hillwalking and climbing all over the country, and has – among other feats – "bagged" (reached the summit of) around 170 Munros (Scottish mountains with an elevation of more than 3,000 feet, or 914 metres). These walks often take 11-12 hours to complete, covering hundreds of miles of untamed terrain in all seasons and weather conditions. "It's all those days that feed back into my work," he said. "But I try and paint my experience of being in the Highlands and on mountains, rather than painting a traditional picture of a place. I think this lends itself very, very well to the nature of the Scottish Highlands, to its atmospheric qualities, its textural qualities." Carefully designed museums and galleries, however, are fraught with needless, manmade barriers which exclude him, when even the wilderness does not.

It's not just that the freedom to spontaneously explore cultural products is limited by only a small percentage being made accessible. Another problem, Keith explains, is that all too often the measures taken to try and help blind people engage with visual art create an experience which is othering and exclusive, rather than inclusive. This was the problem he faced when road-testing a prototype tool designed by Microsoft Research in 2015. Called "Eyes-Free Art", the project made use of cameras which could detect the exact location of a person in relation to a piece of art, and so play different audio tracks triggered by proximity.

"It was good – but it was brutal," Keith said. "My gut reaction was that it had the same feel to it as a white cane. I've noticed that there are many visually impaired people who struggle but won't use a white cane, because it says: 'I'm blind.' And ["Eyes-Free Art"] had this kind of quality to it – that 'this is especially designed for blind people'."

Though well intentioned, it's easy to see what Keith means. In videos of people exploring the project, test subjects grope wildly and conspicuously at the air in front of them, which – if it were to occur in a museum or gallery space – would inescapably draw attention to their disability in a way many do not want.[13] These gestures are, in actuality, functional: they activate either sound effects or audio tracks which modulate in volume and texture based on where in the visual field the subject is pointing. These tracks included sound effects for objects in the piece, and even synthesised sounds representing the primary colours and showing where and how intensely they were mixed.[14] But as contributors to a 2018 volume of *Disability Studies Quarterly* noted of touch tours for the blind, this kind of accessible experience – functional or not – "risks enacting a freak show of otherness".[15]

Keith's feedback to "Eyes-Free Art" made an impact. It led to the evolution of a fresh project, using Microsoft's technological starting point to create something original, immersive, and inclusive for everyone, rather than simply using the tool to render existing works of art accessible to the blind. For this new opus, Keith embarked on a road trip around Oregon, and produced three large-scale works of art depicting different levels of the Hell's Canyon, North America's deepest river gorge. These images were exhibited in a space bristling with finely-tuned, proximity-aware cameras, which would then cue audio tracks recorded at the canyon. In the Oregon Project, audio was not a specialist add-on just for visitors who didn't see – it flowed equally around everyone who visited the work as an intrinsic part of the experience.

Keith's favourite piece of feedback on this experiment in inclusive art came from a blind Microsoft employee who visited the Oregon Project with his wife, daughter, and guide dog. This man spent a long time at the exhibition, and afterwards sought Keith out. "[He said that] he used to go to exhibitions to be with his wife and daughter, and he would get hardly anything out of it. Then someone would say: 'Oh, this is for blind people.' Then he would have his own special audio experiences of the works, which was just for him, or other blind people. So he said that the thing he loved about what we'd done was that he could go there with his family, and it didn't matter that he couldn't see anything. It allowed him to be part of something that his wife and daughter were experiencing."

Sound is one way to bridge the gap between audiences who see and those who don't – another is touch. Fayen d'Evie – an artist, writer, and publisher based in the bushland of southeastern Australia – has striven to use her work to repair the relationship between us all and tactile engagement with art. Her most recent exhibition, as both curator and contributor (entitled *We get in touch with things at the point they break down // Even in the absence of spectators and audiences, dust circulates...* and held in a Melbourne gallery over July and August 2021), explored the theme of haptic – as well as visually aesthetic – beauty.

One collaborative piece consisted of three objects bundled in pieces of cloth Fayen inherited from her grandmother, who died before Fayen was born. The first object is a bronze sculpture by artist Sophie Takách of the space between two people's clasped hands. The second object is a 14cm-long bronze fragment of braille poetry reading "and on and on and on" ("I love this because it's a simple way to introduce people, especially kids, to braille – they can very quickly understand and read out the phrase."). The third object is a piece of jurassic marble, so soft that particles of dust – containing the bones of ancient, compressed creatures – come away on the hands of those who touch it. "To me, it's a profound feeling. We pretend as if works are pristine and perfect, and not ascribed to anybody but an artist, when the reality is that they are made up of all sorts of people who've contributed, whether they're fabricators or whether they're within the body of the material."

Fayen does not seek to rehabilitate touch in the context of exhibited art purely for the sake of making it accessible to the blind: it has value for everyone, she argues. "There are so many more ways that we can be talking about the world, that we can be encountering artwork. To just limit it to visual means of encountering and remembering is really narrowing society's potential for engaging with these works. So I'm interested in bringing conversations into a contemporary gallery space about touch, about these habits or norms that have grown up, where they come from, and also the possibilities that we have for unfurling some of them."

These "habits and norms" – whereby gazing at art from a demarcated distance (sometimes through glass) is normative, and to touch the works is both objectively forbidden and subjectively transgressive – have more sinister origins than we are led to believe. It is in fact not all about protection and conservation, but a taboo born of 19th century social shifts linked to race, gender, and class control, with a distinct colonial element.

Prior to these shifts, tactile encounters with art were part and parcel of the 18th century museum experience. This was true to the point that cultural historian Constance Classen has noted: "To be invited to peruse a collection of exotic artifacts or *objets d'art* and *not* touch anything would be like being invited to someone's home for dinner and not touching the food."[16] Just to perceive these cultural products visually was to be granted only the most shallow form of access, as sight was – in the words of German philosopher Johann Gottfried Herder (1744-1803) – "a superficial sense which can only render the surfaces and colours of objects".[17] To engage via touch was such an intrinsic part of "seeing" an exhibit that 18th century museum visitors would complain of not having a satisfactory viewing if handling were not permitted.[18]

This all changed with the rapid emergence of a middle class with wealth to protect, and so touch became linked with anxieties over theft or damage.[19] Prudish Victorian sensibilities, exacerbated by fresh paranoia over invisible diseases, further vilified tactile encounters with art and artefacts by the uncivilised, unsanitary masses.[20] Touch also became wrapped up in gender politics. Women were associated with the "lower", "animal" senses of taste, touch, and smell, as both sensual and domestic beings; men, on the other hand, were linked to the "higher", "spiritual" senses of sight and hearing.[21] By the dawn of the 20th century, touch had become – according to British psychologist Havelock Ellis (1859 – 1939) – "the least intellectual and least aesthetic" sense.[22] These exclusionary new values and behavioural codes, which were held up as exemplars of good taste and etiquette, were then exported around the world via colonialism. They are now so entrenched that museum staff and visitors will, quite naturally and spontaneously, duplicate them, unless those in positions of power mount active challenges to the status quo.[23]

We need these challenges, because not interrogating hands-off policies – which normalise relying purely on sight to experience most forms of art – cuts us all off from an entire sensory world which could enhance our understanding and appreciation of culture. As things stand, the tactile riches of the world's public collections languish largely unacknowledged, and we've been trained not to notice. Audio descriptions of artworks paint verbal pictures of colours and shapes and other features the blind can't see – but descriptive materials for the sighted don't bother to elucidate on what these visitors can't feel. Is this sculpture cool to the touch – and does it warm up when held in a hand? What does vellum feel like? The modern age has decided it doesn't really care to tell us, or for us to find out.

In the case of the blind, these practices significantly limit access to cultural products and everything they signify. Touch tours for visitors with sight loss may exist at major museums and galleries, but their exclusive, segregational nature serves only to hammer home the fact that the blind are a marginal group, ostracised by the needless supremacy of the sense of sight in these spaces. These tours aren't intended to unlock the riches of tactile engagement with art, or they would be open to everyone.

So thorough is our indoctrination with the idea that touching art is wrong that even when it is expressly permitted, we feel uncomfortable and reluctant to breach such an established social norm.[24] This is true not only of audiences, but of those with a custodial role regarding the artworks. "Touch has been so excluded from the gallery that you can't expect to create tactile works, put them in a gallery, and have staff understand how to engage with them," said Fayen. As a result, she employs "scores" as accompaniments to her work, offering suggestions on how to investigate each piece's tactile qualities ("People can obviously do whatever they like, but the scores are offered as entry points into touch, invitations to engage through touch.").

These scores are not bland, clinical instructions designed to meet minimal accessibility requirements. Rather, they are personal, lyrical explorations of haptic aesthetics, blending beauty and function in a way that enriches these encounters for everyone. "As Erica Fretwell cautions, / in the world of touch, / to read is to erase, / erasure as an act of inscription, / that wears away at fragile dots, / while depositing oils and skin cells. / To read by touch is a form of / autobiographical anno-tation. / Sensing peripheries, / self-sensing peripheries," reads one score, written by Melbourne-based artist and writer Lizzie Boon.[25] These scores are powerful demon-strations of the fact that touch – and instruction on how to touch – need not be just some small, dispassionate way to compensate for what blind people are so tragically missing out on. It can be art in its own right.

This is true of other ways of making art accessible, too. Audio description (AD) in films and TV programmes could easily transcend its roots as assistive afterthought and become an integrated and aesthetic part of the creative whole. Think of its capacity to be beautiful and entertaining if composed by poets or comedians, for example. As things stand, however, all of its imaginative potential remains untapped, because the film and media industries fail to take it seriously.

At present, AD is about as far removed from the creative process of filmmaking as it can be. As Professor Hannah Thompson from Royal Holloway, University of London, notes in a 2018 essay on the subject, AD tracks are created "by specialist companies who do not necessarily share, or perhaps even understand, the director's artistic vision".[26] They are then tacked on to a finished project, which may or may not have left enough silences for an emotionless voice to fill with flat, neutral descriptions of relevant features the sighted eye can see. It's no wonder AD is still only used by a small audience for whom it's essential: the way it's treated is so sterile and unimaginative that it's a chore to switch it on, not the way to amplify a cinematic experience that it could be. This makes it all the more othering: blind people aren't always watching films and TV shows alone – so why hasn't AD been thought of in the context of an experience shared by a group of people, some blind and some sighted? Why give it minimal value for the few when it could so easily have value for everyone?

Fundamentally, part of the reason that AD isn't better than it is now is that we've been trained to perceive certain art forms – like cinema, paintings, and other untouchable museum exhibits – as *necessarily, inherently* visual. We believe the blind lack something so crucial to the experience that there's no point improving on feeble and uninspired accessibility measures. Any alternative kind of sensory engagement could only ever be the palest imitation of sight, so high a pedestal does it sit on – so why try too hard to compensate, if it's ultimately impossible to do so?

This way of thinking is dangerous. It fuels the falsehood that vision is the only important sense we have, encouraging us all to squander the power and potential applications of the others. It assumes the blind are completely divorced from any experience of vision, reinforcing the myth that blindness is one, uniform thing (all-encompassing blackness), rather than a diverse spectrum of experiences. Most dangerous of all, it creates yet another self-fulfilling prophecy of deprivation and separation. The irony is that if we keep thinking of the blind as utterly divorced from the visual arts, and use that as an excuse for poor access, we create the very systems and practices that are actually responsible.

If anything epitomises the fact that we really do think of the blind as cut off from the visual world, it's the experiences of artists with sight loss. "There's a separate set of standards if you're blind," Keith said. "There are different expectations. It's almost like when people hear that you're registered blind, you can't be a professional. You have to be an amateur. Your prices must be cheap.

And a lot of this is about people's thinking – they think you can't be a proper painter. It's soul-destroying, and very, very problematic that people don't take you seriously, and it's probably one of the things that depresses me the most."

The truth is that if we should be taking anything from the visual arts, it's the value of diverse viewpoints – not the devaluing of them. Great art is all about seeing differently, and celebrating it. The French Impressionists, for example, used broken-up areas of brilliant colour applied with fast strokes of the brush, demonstrating the beauty of the blur and that colour is subjective, not objective. From their works, we can gain a better understanding of what central vision loss and colour blindness really look like. Abstract artists, like Wassily Kandinsky or Kusama Yayoi, offer us windows into what it is to see dots, patterns, after-imaging, and floating panels of coloration, all of which characterise various eye conditions. Non-normative vision is not, in fact, some niche obscurity in the annals of art history: rather, it is a major and enduring theme. We should think of the visual arts as a tool to better conceptualise the idea of a spectrum of blindness and sight , rather than using them to reinforce myths of black-and-white absolutes.

Moreover, real-life blindness and non-normative ways of seeing have engendered some of the world's most beloved and ubiquitous paintings, by some of the greatest artists. Claude Monet had cataracts for almost two decades, and continued painting throughout that period.[27] It has long been theorised that Vincent Van Gogh had problems with his eyesight (his liberal use of yellows and swirling haloes of light are visual symptoms associated with a number of causes, including glaucoma, over-zealous treatment with a medication called digitalis, and too much absinthe).[28] Leonardo Da Vinci likely had intermittent strabismus, meaning his eyes were aligned abnormally, so could move independently of one another.[29]

We think of blindness as separate from visual art – and yet, when we go to galleries and museums, or buy posters for our homes, or search for art online to inspire and educate us, it is blind perspectives – and other non-normative ways of seeing – that we crave. We need to recognise this hypocrisy, and that these truths have been so well hidden to so many, and deemed so unimportant to their narrative. Why is it that we can celebrate diverse viewpoints when they hang resplendent before us in gold frames, but not when they are another human being's optical reality?

Perhaps the best example to convince us to change the way we think is that of the Romantic painter J. M. W. Turner (1775-1851). When we look at his work today, we are seeing radically different paintings to those the artist created – and these changes in perception between his time and our own mirror a real-life journey into sight loss. Turner was famous for working with pigments which he knew looked their best when freshly applied (several shades, like cochineal carmine and chrome yellow, faded even within his lifetime), and stored his paintings in extremely damp places, leading to mould, discolouration, and flaking.[30] As a result, skies once coloured with short-lived natural indigo (which he mixed with black or vermilion) now spread in grey or reddish tones across canvases streaked and stained by time and environment.[31]

We all experience sight loss with Turner's paintings – and yet he is one of the most beloved and enduringly celebrated painters in history. His 1839 work *The Fighting Temeraire* was voted Britain's greatest painting in a poll hosted by BBC Radio 4 in 2005.[32] Statues of the artist positively litter London landmarks, from the Victoria and Albert Museum to St Paul's Cathedral. He's the face of the polymer £20 note, and has lit up the silver screen in the Oscar-nominated film, *Mr Turner* (2014).

The lesson here is that all ways of seeing are valid – including those of people with sight loss. A blind person's appreciation of visual art is just as legitimate as a sighted person's, just as the world's love of Turner is legitimate. By creating problems of access, however, we are failing to validate blind engagement with art as a phenomenon, and constructing a false narrative that there is one, true, correct way to see art: objectively, with 20/20 vision. But art, by its very nature, can never be objective. It is as much linked to engaging on an emotional level as it is about the appearance of an object, for both artist and audience. Picasso put it best: "Painting is a blind man's profession. He paints not what he sees, but what he feels, what he tells himself about what he has seen."[33]

Those words have never been better illustrated than by the story of Park Hwan, a painter based in Chuncheon City, in Gangwon province, South Korea. In the autumn of 2013, Hwan was preparing to exhibit as a part of the Korea International Art Fair when he was involved in a major traffic collision. Returning home after three months in hospital, Hwan was devastated at the thought that blindness meant he could no longer be a visual artist. "I had not yet accepted in my heart that the world, which had been so natural to me, was now all of a sudden invisible," he said. "In a lot of pain, I sat on the sofa all day and cried. I thought that I couldn't draw anymore. Every day was like hell and my frustration grew."

But around August 2014, Hwan asked his family to bring him a canvas. "It was sad that I couldn't see, but I didn't want to stop making my beloved paintings. At first it was dark and difficult to figure out what, where, and how to position things, and how to express a sense of mixed colours, and I failed over and over. It felt impossible, and I thought about giving up countless times. But then I started thinking that I could use my own hands instead of a brush, and I also remembered the wool my mother always had by her side for knitting, and thought I could use that to replace the sketch."

From these beginnings, Hwan developed what would become his signature style. First, he makes a preliminary sketch using thread, held at points with sewing pins. This framework is then reinforced with thicker threads and other materials, including scraps of denim, soil, and tree bark. Oil paint is then applied to this three-dimensional base using the tips of the fingers.

As well as provoking physical changes in his artistic process, blindness also dramatically transformed Hwan's emotional relationship with his work. "In the past, when I was not blind, I lived only for my own success. I wanted to be recognised as a great artist, so that my honour would be elevated, and I was trying to advance my career abroad when I had my accident. After that, when I opened my eyes, I saw only a world of darkness. I think it was like being born again and beginning a new life. I started to see other people's pain that I hadn't noticed before. So now I hope to be an artist whose work gives warm comfort and hope to people who are suffering with pain and sorrow. Now, my goal is to be able to express a brighter tomorrow."

The brighter tomorrow Hwan portrays is at once beautiful, poignant, and charged with heartfelt emotion.

One painting, entitled *Open-Minded World* (2017), illustrates the artist's shift in perspective which transformed the dark days of the accident's aftermath into "a brighter world, with beautiful flowers and clear water, unfolding before my eyes". Another painting, *Life of an Old Tree* (2018), symbolises Hwan himself, and the infinite resilience of the human spirit in the face of great and turbulent change: the aged, rotting branches are stippled with fresh buds and intertwined with wildflowers. ("The old tree is still alive, just as I did not give up and had hope.")

Hwan's paintings capture the greatest and most unique qualities humans are capable of – empathy, resilience, and future-looking hope – and he expresses them without using his eyes. His story perfectly showcases that emotional engagement is the true energy at work in artistic practice, and it will always trump the visual experience (as Descartes once wrote, it is "the soul which sees, and not the eye").[34] His is exactly the art we should celebrate, because it epitomises the very best of us. And if anything demonstrates that the blind painter is as connected to the global tapestry of visual art as anyone else, it's that Hwan applies paint to his masterpieces of feeling with his fingertips – just as our ancestors did, in a dark, wet, Indonesian cave, 44,000 years ago.

Afterword

Now that you are coming to the end of *Blind Spot,* which ultimately only skims the surface of a topic that could fill countless more books, I hope the question on your mind is – what next? Now that I know better, how can I be better?

There are, of course, tangible and quantifiable ways you can adapt. You can empower the organisations making a difference in blind people's lives by changing your spending habits. Charities for the blind exist all around the world and do amazing work which often won't get done otherwise – work like transcribing books into braille, offering emotional support and daily living advice to those experiencing sight loss, and selling assistive technology and other everyday gadgets. They also champion the rights of the blind in law, and promote the visibility of blind people and issues in the media.

If you are in the UK, you can find a helpful (but not comprehensive) list of relevant charities on the Royal College of Ophthalmologists website.[1] This list can also give you a sense of how broad a spectrum of services are available – from those offering support for veterans to those tailored to specific eye conditions, no matter how rare; from those whose priority is funding scientific research to those that distribute medical resources to the world at large via hospital ships. Many people are also unaware that guide dog training is a charitable endeavour. Guide Dogs for the Blind (in the UK) rely on donations to continue their work, which can drastically improve blind people's independence and wellbeing – and you can sponsor a puppy in training for as little as £1 a week.[2]

You can embrace the accessibility features on social media platforms, and make them a part of your daily routine. Write alt text for images on Instagram, Facebook, and Twitter, keeping in mind that this feature is not the same as writing a caption. Rather, imagine that the image has failed to load and that the alt text must replace it, conveying – as succinctly as possible – any relevant details the sighted eye would see. Capitalise each separate word in a hashtag, so that screen readers can vocalise them correctly. With videos, you don't have to go so far as to incorporate clunky audio description – but let audio and visual storytelling methods work in parallel, so that anyone relying on just one stream isn't missing out. A few small changes are all that's required to make your social media accounts inclusive – and if you work to make them habits, they will be as natural and spontaneous as any other part of your online life.

You can help solve everyday access problems faced by blind people by signing up with the free mobile app Be My Eyes, a brilliant resource which allows the blind to connect via video call with sighted volunteers who can see for them.[3] You can sign up from anywhere in the world, and the app operates in 180 languages.[4]

If you'd rather meet people in person, and you lead an active lifestyle, you can become a guide runner, and accompany blind people on jogs and runs to ensure they're safe. Anyone can train to do this; it requires attending a Sight Loss Awareness and Guide Running workshop, passing a DBS check, and undertaking safe-guarding training.[5] You will then be listed on a national database for blind people in your local area to find you through.

You can keep learning and educating yourself about blindness and blind people. For your next read, why not try *And There Was Light*, the lyrical, expressive autobiog-raphy of Jacques Lusseyran (1924-1971), who – aged just 16 – set up his own French resistance cell in the spring of 1941, and survived 15 months in a Nazi concentration camp? Or perhaps you'd like to learn more about some of the people you may have discovered here – like the traveller James Holman (by means of Jason Roberts' brilliant biography *A Sense of the World*) or musician duo Amadou & Mariam (through the autobiography they wrote together, *Away From the Light of Day*).

Alternatively, if you want a break from non-fiction, you can explore some of the great masterpieces of literature written by blind people. Pick up a copy of the immensely influential poem *Paradise Lost* by John Milton (1608-1674), which Samuel Johnson ranked as among the very highest "productions of the human mind" (it inspired works as diverse as Mary Shelley's *Frankenstein* and Phillip Pullman's *His Dark Materials* trilogy, which even takes its name from a line in the poem).[6] Pullman recommends the audiobook, which best showcases the musicality of the blind Milton's masterpiece ("No one, not even Shakespeare, surpasses Milton in his command of the sound, the music, the weight and taste and texture of English words").[7]

Or for something a little more modern, why not try the short stories of Jorge Luis Borges (1899-1986), whose writing – filled with labyrinths and libraries, tigers, dreams, and mirror images – was so uniquely inventive that critics were forced to coin the term "Borgesian" to describe it, just as they had for the likes of Kafka and Sartre.[8] Borges left such a mark on literature that he has been called the father of the Latin American novel, influencing such writers as Gabriel García Márquez and Mario Vargas Llosa.[9]

You can also play an active role in raising the profile of accomplished blind people from history, whose stories have such power to inspire others and challenge stereotypes of what someone without sight can do. Start conversations about blind people you admire, so that others can be introduced to these figures. Buy their books or artwork or music, so that they – and those following in their footsteps – are culturally and economically validated in their fields. In particular, support the work of blind visual artists and other similar professionals, thereby affirming their legitimacy in careers that the uninformed observer might think rely, inherently on sight.

People often ask me if they should be offering assistance directly to the blind when out and about. There is no hard and fast rule here, but my general advice would be to base your reading of the situation on more than just the fact that the person is blind. Don't assume they need help, or can't do something by themselves, just because they can't see – but equally, if someone looks lost or confused (blind or not), a helping hand might go a long way toward solving a problem or making someone's day a little better. With that in mind, though, I recommend erring on the side of kindness. Better to offer help and be refused than leave someone who is struggling feeling isolated and alone.

Most of all, I encourage you to be curious and critical of the world around you. The burden of being the one to instigate change falls all too often on the marginalised groups themselves, because they are the ones encountering the problem: in reality, we should all be sharing this responsibility among us. So play an active role in redressing the balance: identify the ways in which the world is lacking, and use your imagination to dream up how it could be better (no qualifications required for this – Louis Braille (1809-1852) was just 15 years old when he invented the tactile alphabet of dots which bears his name, and which is still very much in use today). Ask questions, even if you don't think the answers will affect you, because you don't have to be blind to care about blind people's experiences.

I truly believe that everyone wants to be kind – but without knowing we are acting unkindly, we cannot improve ourselves. This is why education is so important. And while I wrote this book largely to educate the sighted majority, in doing so I educated myself, too. I found role models, uncovered data, and retold stories which made me feel proud and celebratory about my blindness. I feel that in many ways I have written the book I wish I could have read when I lost my sight at 19, when I felt that blindness was something I could never love, only come to terms with. Compiling this book has helped me love this part of myself. And everybody deserves the right to love exactly who they are, and be proud of their identity.

I recognise, however, that it is hard work to educate ourselves as adults in areas where society has failed us. We have to be active – we have to scour and search and dig for the information we deserve. Once we find it, it is just as hard to use it to reconfigure the way we think, and to break and reform habits that are woven so tightly into the fabric of our lives. I acknowledge this fact, and in light of it, I thank you for reading this book to the end.

Change is not easy, and realising that something is broken and must be fixed is often the first step on what can be a long and difficult road. But we must hold on to the fact that it is worth it to make these changes. In the words of another brilliant blind person from history – the teacher, poet, and tireless advocate for rights for the blind in Australia, Tilly Aston (1873 – 1947) – "All noble things we do and dare must be fruitful, sometime, somewhere."[10]

All societies have blind spots – but to know that and do nothing is not good enough. We must work to be better, safe in the knowledge that it is always worthwhile to be kind.

References

Introduction

1. "Evolution of the eye." *New Scientist*. www.newscientist.com/term/evolution-of-the-eye/. Accessed 8 October 2021.
2. Scott AW, Bressler NM, Ffolkes S, Wittenborn JS, Jorkasky J. Public Attitudes About Eye and Vision Health. JAMA Ophthalmol. 2016 Oct 1;134(10):1111-1118. doi: 10.1001/jamaophthalmol.2016.2627. PMID: 27490785.
3. Giridhar P, Dandona R, Prasad MN, Kovai V, Dandona L. Fear of blindness and perceptions about blind people. The Andhra Pradesh eye disease study. Indian J Ophthalmol 2002; 50:239. www.ijo.in/article.asp?issn=03014738;year=2002;volume=50;issue=3;spage=239;epage=46;aulast=Giridhar#top. Accessed 8 October 2021.
4. "The Self-Portrait Jorge Luis Borges Drew After Going Blind." Emily Temple, *Lit Hub*, 24 August 2018. lithub.com/the-self-portrait-jorge-luis-borges-drew-after-going-blind/. Accessed 8 October 2021.
5. Ibid.
6. "Shaquille O'Neal adds fuel conspiracy theory after claiming Stevie Wonder 'saw' him in an elevator." *NZ Herald*, 13 December 2019. www.nzherald.co.nz/sport/shaquille-oneal-adds-fuel-conspiracy-theory-after-claiming-stevie-wonder-saw-him-in-an-elevator/CMPOWM2YHEHOHDRO-43JX2XX2LA/. Accessed 8 October 2021.
7. "The Viral Facebook Photo Of A 'Fake' Blind Woman Shows We Still Don't Understand Being Partially Sighted." Ellie Southwood, *Huffington Post*, 31 January 2019. www.huffingtonpost.co.uk/entry/blind-woman-facebook-photo_uk_5c52d232e4b-0ca92c6dd9421. Accessed 8 October 2021.
8. "Ignorance towards blind people being passed from generation to generation." *enable*, 5 March 2015. enablemagazine.co.uk/ignorance-towards-blind-people-being-passed-from-generation-to-generation/. Accessed 8 October 2021.
9. "Eye health and sight loss stats and facts." *RNIB*, April 2018. www.rnib.org.uk/sites/default/files/Eye%20health%20and%20sight%20loss%20stats%20and%20facts.pdf. Accessed 8 October 2021.
10. Ibid.

11. "Avoidable blindness." *Light for the World*. www.light-for-the-world.uk/avoidable-blindness#:~:text=About%2080%20 percent%20of%20blindness%20is%20preventable. Accessed 8 October 2021.
12. "Blindness and vision impairment." *World Health Organisation*, 26 February 2021. www.who.int/news-room/fact-sheets/detail/ blindness-and-visual-impairment. Accessed 8 October 2021.
13. "Key information and statistics on sight loss in the UK." *RNIB*, 1 September 2019. www.rnib.org.uk/professionals/knowledge-and-research-hub/key-information-and-statistics. Accessed 8 October 2021.

Chapter 1: On visibility

1. "Emotional support and confidence." *RNIB*. www.rnib.org.uk/ professionals/knowledge-and-research-hub/research-reports/ emotional-support-and-befriending-research. Accessed 8 October 2021.
2. "Facing blindness alone." *RNIB*. https://www.rnib.org.uk/sites/ default/files/Facing%20blindness%20alone%20Campaign%20 report.pdf. Accessed 8 October 2021.
3. "Coming to terms with sight loss." *RNIB*. www.rnib.org.uk/ recently-diagnosed/coming-terms-sight-loss. Accessed 8 October 2021.
4. "My Voice." *RNIB*. www.rnib.org.uk/sites/default/files/My%20 Voice%202015%20-%20Summary%20-%20Accessible%20 Word_1.docx
5. "Visions of a travelling man." Kevin Rushby, The Guardian, 12 August 2006. www.theguardian.com/books/2006/aug/12/fea-turesreviews.guardianreview13. Accessed 11 October 2021.
6. Jason Roberts, A Sense of the World. Simon & Schuster, 2006. p262-3.
7. Ibid. p263.
8. Ibid. p323.
9. Ibid. p212.
10. Ibid. p291.
11. Ibid. p291-2.
12. Ibid. p292.
13. James Wilson, *Biography of the Blind*. Creative Media Partners, 2019.

14. "My Voice 2015." *RNIB*. www.rnib.org.uk/sites/default/files/My%20Voice%202015%20-%20Full%20report%20-%20Accessible%20PDF_0.pdf. Accessed 8 October 2021.
15. "Hate Crime." *Home Office*. assets.publishing.service.gov.uk/government/uploads/system/uploads/attachment_data/file/839172/hate-crime-1819-hosb2419.pdf. Accessed 8 October 2021.
16. "A PLAY THAT EXPLORES BLINDESS; Benedict Nightingale writes frequently on theatre in London." Benedict Nightingale, *The New York Times*, 27 March 1983. www.nytimes.com/1983/03/27/theater/play-that-explores-blindness-benedict-nightingale-writes-frequently-theater.html. Accessed 8 October 2021.
17. Ibid.
18. Ibid.
19. Ibid.
20. "How blind Victorians campaigned for inclusive education." David Turner, *BBC News*, 1 October 2014. www.bbc.co.uk/news/blogs-ouch-29327232. Accessed 8 October 2021.
21. Old Red Lion Theatre, www.oldredliontheatre.co.uk/iqs/dbitemid.108/rp.1/sfa.view/all-events.html. Accessed 8 October 2021.
22. Sheilah Graham, *Beloved Infidel: The Education of a Woman*. Holt, 1958.
23. "Nicholas Saunderson FRS." *The Royal Society*. royalsociety.org/topics-policy/diversity-in-science/scientists-with-disabilities/nicholas-saunderson/. Accessed 8 October 2021.
24. Referenced as Baker 18971 on p361 of this PDF: core.ac.uk/download/pdf/82454029.pdf. Accessed 8 October 2021.
25. "Blind Jack." Charlie Clissitt, *Historic UK*. www.historic-uk.com/HistoryUK/HistoryofEngland/Blind-Jack/. Accessed 8 October 2021.
26. "The story of Blind Jack – the man who built Britain's roads." *Telegraph*, 15 August 2016. www.telegraph.co.uk/only-in-britain/road-builder-john-metcalf-born/. Accessed 8 October 2021.
27. "Leonhard Euler." *MacTutor*. mathshistory.st-andrews.ac.uk/Biographies/Euler/. Accessed 8 October 2021.
   "Eulogy of Leonhard Euler by Nicolas Fuss." *MacTutor*. mathshistory.st-andrews.ac.uk/Extras/Euler_Fuss_Eulogy/. Accessed 8 October 2021.
28. "Employment research." *RNIB*. www.rnib.org.uk/professionals/

knowledge-and-research-hub/research-reports/employment-research. Accessed 8 October 2021.

29. "Eye health and sight loss stats and facts." *RNIB*, April 2018. www.rnib.org.uk/sites/default/files/Eye%20health%20and%20sight%20loss%20stats%20and%20facts.pdf. Accessed 8 October 2021.

30. "Anne's Formative Years (1866-1886)." *Braille Bug*. braillebug.org/hkgallery.asp?frameid=74. Accessed 8 October 2021.

31. "Helen Keller." *Perkins*. www.perkins.org/history/people/helen-keller. Accessed 8 October 2021.

32. "Amadou and Mariam: 'When you live in this world you have to make yourself useful'." Caspar Llewellyn Smith, *The Guardian*, 26 February 2012. www.theguardian.com/music/2012/feb/26/amadou-and-mariam-bamako-interview. Accessed 8 October 2021.

33. Ibid.

Chapter 2: On accessibility

1. "London's Policy for Accessible Pedestrian Crossings." Inclusivity Maker. www.inclusivecitymaker.com/london-audible-signals-pedestrian-crossings/. Accessed 8 October 2021.

2. Ibid.

3. "The secret button at pedestrian crossings." BBC News, 29 May 2013. www.bbc.co.uk/news/blogs-ouch-22706881. Accessed 8 October 2021.

4. ""Who put that there!"" RNIB. www.rnib.org.uk/sites/default/files/Who%20put%20that%20there%21%20Report%20February%202015.pdf. Accessed 8 October 2021.

5. Hyungkyoo Kim & Dongwook Sohn (2020) The urban built environment and the mobility of people with visual impairments: analysing the travel behaviours based on mobile phone data, Journal of Asian Architecture and Building Engineering, 19:6, 731-741, DOI: 10.1080/13467581.2020.1779727

6. "Three in four guide dog owners illegally refused service." RNIB. 13 June 2019. www.rnib.org.uk/about-us/media-centre/latest-media-releases/guide-dog-owners-illegally-refused-service. Accessed 8 October 2021.

7. "Planes Trains and Canes." YouTube. www.youtube.com/channel/UCUAGEcdoYLOD7x5hTDKmVoA. Accessed 8 October 2021.

8. "Disability." World Health Organisation. www.who.int/
    health-topics/disability#tab=tab_1. Accessed 8 October 2021.
9. Ibid.
10. "Dr. Temple Grandin of CSU Named One of the Top 10
    College Professors in the Country." Temple Grandin. www.
    templegrandin.com. Accessed 8 October 2021.
11. www.gutenberg.org. Accessed 8 October 2021.
12. "A brief history of OCR: the technology inside your
    ScanMarker." ScanMarker, 2 April 2019. scanmarker.
    com/2019/04/02/a-brief-history-of-ocr-the-technology-inside-
    your-scanmarker/. Accessed 8 October 2021.
13. Ibid.
14. "How our unconscious visual biases change the way we perceive
    objects." Beverley Pickard-Jones, The Conversation, 15 January
    2019. theconversation.com/how-our-unconscious-visual-biases-
    change-the-way-we-perceive-objects-109039. Accessed 8 October
    2021.
15. Krosch, Amy R, and David M Amodio. "Scarcity disrupts the
    neural encoding of Black faces: A socioperceptual pathway to
    discrimination." Journal of personality and social psychology vol.
    117,5 (2019): 859-875. doi:10.1037/pspa0000168, "Economic
    scarcity shifts perception, leads to discrimination." James Dean,
    Cornell Chronicle, 28 October 2019. news.cornell.edu/sto-
    ries/2019/10/economic-scarcity-shifts-perception-leads-discrimi-
    nation. Accessed 8 October 2021.
16. Tactile Universe. tactileuniverse.org. Accessed 8 October 2021.
17. "How a blind astronomer found a way to hear the stars." Wanda
    Diaz Merced, TED, 2016. www.ted.com/talks/wanda_diaz_
    merced_how_a_blind_astronomer_found_a_way_to_hear_the_
    stars?language=en. Accessed 8 October 2021.
18. "Wanda Díaz-Merced." The Royal Society. royalsociety.org/
    topics-policy/diversity-in-science/scientists-with-disabilities/wan-
    da-diaz-merced/. Accessed 8 October 2021.
19. Ibid.
20. "Karl Jansky and his Merry-go-Round." National Radio
    Astronomy Observatory. public.nrao.edu/gallery/karl-jan-
    sky-and-his-merrygoround/. Accessed 8 October 2021.
21. "The 4 ways sound affects us." Julian Treasure, 2009. www.ted.
    com/talks/julian_treasure_the_4_ways_sound_affects_us?lan-
    guage=en. Accessed 8 October 2021.
22. "Listen up: the potential profits from the podcast boom." Fed-

erica Tedeschi, Citywire Selector, 24 March 2021. citywireselec-tor.com/news/listen-up-the-potential-profits-from-the-podcast-boom/a1484809. Accessed 8 October 2021.

23. "Takadanobaba Station." Japan Travel, 20 June 2013. en.japan-travel.com/tokyo/takadanobaba-station/5096. Accessed 8 October 2021.

24. "In Tokyo, These Trains Jingle All the Way." YouTube, uploaded by Great Big Story, 3 August 2018. www.youtube.com/watch?v=nSG5IkRA9BE. Accessed 8 October 2021.

25. "Music in Japanese train stations." A.L., Japan Experience, 18 May 2016. www.japan-experience.com/to-know/understand-ing-japan/music-in-japanese-stations. Accessed 8 October 2021.

26. "Departure melodies: Celebrating the jingles' contribution to the rail experience in Japan." Russell Thomas, The Japan Times, 15 June 2019. www.japantimes.co.jp/life/2019/06/15/lifestyle/departure-melodies-celebrating-jingles-contribution-rail-experi-ence-japan/. Accessed 8 October 2021.

27. "Disordinary Architecture." The Disordinary Architecture Proj-ect. disordinaryarchitecture.co.uk. Accessed 8 October 2021.

28. "About the Founder." PAC. www.pac.bz/about/. Accessed 8 October 2021.

Chapter 3: On culture

1. www.npg.org.uk. Accessed 11 October 2021.

2. Ibid.

3. www.nationaltheatre.org.uk/your-visit/access/audio-de-scribed-performances. Accessed 11 October 2021.
   "Audio Described Performances." Official London Theatre. https://officiallondontheatre.com/access/audio/. Accessed 11 October 2021.

4. "Braille books." RNIB. https://www.rnib.org.uk/reading-ser-vices/books/braille-books. Accessed 11 October 2021.,
   "European Book Publishing Statistics." Federation of Euro-pean Publisher, 29 November 2012. web.archive.org/web/20131019134556/http://www.sne.fr/img/pdf/Doc%20pour%20Flash%20et%20Lettre/European-book-publish-ing-stat2011.pdf. Accessed 11 October 2021.

5. "Facts and figures of the British Library." British Library. www.bl.uk/about-us/our-story/facts-and-figures-of-the-british-library. Accessed 11 October 2021.

6. "A Journey to the Oldest Cave Paintings in the World." Jo Marchant, Smithsonian Magazine, January 2016. www.smithsonianmag.com/history/journey-oldest-cave-paintings-world-180957685/. Accessed 11 October 2021.

7. "Earliest music instruments found." BBC News, 25 May 2012. www.bbc.co.uk/news/science-environment-18196349. Accessed 11 October 2021.

8. Ibid.

9. "Picasso's African-influenced Period - 1907 to 1909." www.pablopicasso.org/africanperiod.jsp. Accessed 11 October 2021.

10. "Tapestry replica of Picasso's anti-war masterpiece Guernica removed from United Nations headquarters after 35 years." Kabir Jhala, The Art Newspaper, 26 February 2021. www.theartnewspaper.com/news/guernica-tapestry-based-of-picasso-s-monumental-anti-war-masterpiece-removed-from-united-nations-headquarters. Accessed 11 October 2021.

11. Ibid.

12. "Did The Rite of Spring really spark a riot?" Ivan Hewett, BBC News, 29 May 2013. www.bbc.co.uk/news/magazine-22691267. Accessed 11 October 2021.

13. "Eyes-Free Art: Exploring Proxemic Audio Interfaces for Blind and Low Vision Art Engagement." Microsoft, 22 February 2020. www.microsoft.com/en-us/research/video/eyes-free-art-exploring-proxemic-audio-interfaces-blind-low-vision-art-engagement-2/. Accessed 11 October 2021.

14. Ibid.

15. D'Evie, Fayen; Kleege, Georgina. (2018). The Gravity, The Levity: Let Us Speak of Tactile Encounter. Disability Studies Quarterly. Vol 38, No 3. DOI: http://dx.doi.org/10.18061/dsq.v38i3.6483. Accessed 11 October 2021.

16. "Living in Three Dimensions." Deborah Kent, Braille Monitor, June 2016. nfb.org/images/nfb/publications/bm/bm16/bm1606/bm160608.htm. Accessed 11 October 2021.

17. Ibid.

18. Yerxa, Donald. (2013). The Deepest Sense: An Interview with Constance Classen. Historically Speaking. 14. 27-28. DOI: http://doi.org/10.1353/hsp.2013.0030. Accessed 11 October 2021.

19. "Living in Three Dimensions." Deborah Kent, Braille Monitor, June 2016. nfb.org/images/nfb/publications/bm/bm16/bm1606/bm160608.htm. Accessed 11 October 2021.

20. Ibid.
21. Excerpt from Constance Classen's "Introduction" to The Color of Angels: Cosmology, Gender and the Aesthetic Imagination (London and New York: Routledge, 1998). www.david-howes.com/senses/Classen.htm. Accessed 11 October 2021.
22. Fretwell, Erica. (2013). Stillness Is a Move: Helen Keller and the Kinaesthetics of Autobiography. American Literary History. Vol 25, No 3. 563-587. academic.oup.com/alh/article-abstract/25/3/563/121061. Accessed 11 October 2021.
23. Coffee, Kevin. (2008). Cultural inclusion, exclusion and the formative roles of museums, Museum Management and Curatorship. Vol 23, No 3. 261-279. DOI: https://doi.org/10.1080/09647770802234078. Accessed 11 October 2021.
24. D'Evie, Fayen; Kleege, Georgina. (2018). The Gravity, The Levity: Let Us Speak of Tactile Encounter. Disability Studies Quarterly. Vol 38, No 3. DOI: http://dx.doi.org/10.18061/dsq.v38i3.6483. Accessed 11 October 2021.
25. "LIZZIE BOON | JENNIFER JUSTICE "SCORES"." offsite. westspace.org.au/work/scores-3/. Accessed 11 October 2021.
26. Thompson, Hannah. (2018). Audio Description: Turning Access to Film into Cinema Art. Disability Studies Quarterly. Vol 38, No 3. dsq-sds.org/article/view/6487/5085. Accessed 11 October 2021.
27. "Claude Monet's Health." C. Monet Gallery. www.cmonetgallery.com/cataracts.aspx. Accessed 11 October 2021.
28. "Van Gogh's Eyesight and Paintings." The Eye Associates, 7 March 2016. www.theeyeassociates.com/van-goghs-eyesight-and-how-it-may-have-influenced-his-paintings/. Accessed 11 October 2021.
29. Tyler, Christopher W. (2019). Evidence That Leonardo da Vinci Had Strabismus. JAMA Ophthalmol. Vol 137, No 1. 82–86. DOI:10.1001/jamaophthalmol.2018.3833. Accessed 11 October 2021.
30. "Palettes of the masters: JMW Turner." Winsor & Newton. www.winsornewton.com/row/articles/art-history/palettes-masters-jmw-turner/. Accessed 11 October 2021.
31. Ibid.
32. "The Fighting Temeraire voted the Greatest Painting in Britain." BBC Press Office, 5 September 2005. www.bbc.co.uk/pressoffice/pressreleases/stories/2005/09_september/05/painting.shtml. Accessed 11 October 2021.

33. "Painting is a blind mans [sic] profession he paints not." Course Hero. www.coursehero.com/file/p25skqeb/Painting-is-a-blind-mans-profession-He-paints-not-what-he-sees-but-what-he/. Accessed 11 October 2021.
34. "Why you should re-read Paradise Lost." Benjamin Ramm, BBC Culture, 19 April 2017. www.bbc.com/culture/article/20170419-why-paradise-lost-is-one-of-the-worlds-most-important-poems. Accessed 11 October 2021.

Afterword

1. "Charities." The Royal College of Ophthalmologists. www.rcophth.ac.uk/patients/links-to-charities/. Accessed 11 October 2021.
2. "Sponsor a puppy." Guide Dogs. www.guidedogs.org.uk/sponsor-a-puppy-today/. Accessed 11 October 2021.
3. "Sighted Volunteer." Be My Eyes. support.bemyeyes.com/hc/en-us/categories/360000920938-Sighted-Volunteer. Accessed 11 October 2021.
4. "Our story." Be My Eyes. www.bemyeyes.com/about. Accessed 11 October 2021.
5. "Become a Guide Runner." England Athletics. www.englandathletics.org/athletics-and-running/our-programmes/find-a-guide/become-a-guide-runner/. Accessed 11 October 2021.
6. "Why you should re-read Paradise Lost." Benjamin Ramm, BBC Culture, 19 April 2017. www.bbc.com/culture/article/20170419-why-paradise-lost-is-one-of-the-worlds-most-important-poems. Accessed 11 October 2021.
7. Ibid.
8. "Jorge Luis Borges." Poetry Foundation. www.poetryfoundation.org/poets/jorge-luis-borges. Accessed 11 October 2021.
9. "Is Borges the 20th Century's most important writer?" Jane Ciabattari, BBC Culture, 2 September 2014. www.bbc.com/culture/article/20140902-the-20th-centurys-best-writer. Accessed 11 October 2021.
10. "Tilly Aston—Australia's First Blind Teacher, Poet & Visionary." Maribel Steel, Vision Aware. visionaware.org/everyday-living/essential-skills/vision-rehabilitation-services/other-vision-rehabilitation-professionals/tilly-aston-australias-first-blind-teacher-poet-and-visionary/. Accessed 11 October 2021.

Appendix

Below is a list of everyone interviewed in this book in order of appearance, and how you can learn more about them and their work.

Amadou Bagayoko and Mariam Doumbia
- Official website: http://www.amadou-mariam.com
- Music available to stream on all players
- You can read their 2010 co-written autobiography, *Away From The Light of Day* [print only]

Mandy Redvers-Rowe
- Twitter handle: @MandyRRowe
- The Disordinary Architecture Project official website: https://disordinaryarchitecture.co.uk

Michele Mele
- You can order Michele's book at this link: https://www.amazon.it/Luniverso-Storie-scienziati-ipovedenti-vedenti/dp/8833812383 [Italian only]

Mona Minkara
- Twitter handle: @mona_minkara
- Official website: https://monaminkara.com
- "Planes, Trains, & Canes" on YouTube: https://www.youtube.com/channel/UCUAGEcdoYLOD7x5hTDKmVoA

Nicolas Bonne
- Twitter handle: @coffee_samurai
- Tactile Universe Project official website: https://tactileuniverse.org

Sina Bahram
- Twitter handle: @SinaBahram
- Official website: https://www.sinabahram.com
- Prime Access Consulting: https://www.pac.bz [has a Resources tab with lots of information on web accessibility and inclusive design]

Keith Salmon
- Official website (including artworks for sale): https://www.keithsalmon.org
- Sales enquiries may also be directed to Keith via: e-mail: keith@keithsalmon.org

Fayen d'Evie
- Official website: https://fayendevie.com
- Instagram handle: @muckletimes

Park Hwan
- Official blog: https://blog.naver.com/hihwan1112 [Korean only]
- Sales enquiries can be directed to Hwan [in Korean] via the above blog, or email: hihwan1112@naver.com

Acknowledgements

I firstly want to thank all my interviewees (Amy Bower, Sina Bahram, Mona Minkara, Millie Knight, Keith Salmon, Michele Mele, Tsujii Nobuyuki, Nicolas Bonne, Christine Ha, Park Hwan, Mandy Redvers-Rowe, Amadou Bagayoko, Michelle Anne Holman, and Fayen d'Evie). Even if their words are not specifically quoted, every conversation I had with this diverse range of brilliant and accomplished people informed what and how I wrote. I'm immensely grateful for their time, and hope with all my heart that they enjoy – and feel faithfully represented in – this book.

Thank you also to those who facilitated and assisted with interviews in various ways (Kobayashi Mio, Georgia Villar) and in particular to my dear friend Park Jaehyun, who translated for Park Hwan.

Thank you to my family, who support me, always, and in everything. Particular thanks to my grandpa Clive – my first disabled role model, who has taught me so much – and my mum, my most patient and tireless proofreader. Thanks also to the family I have chosen – my partner Alex – who is also endlessly patient, and my go-to sounding board for ideas. I love you all very, very much.

Finally, a huge thank you to Heather and Laura at 404 Ink, who have worked so tirelessly to make this project happen, and with whom it was such a pleasure to work.

Anyone who has known me a long time will know that writing books has always been my ultimate dream. I want to convey to absolutely everyone who played even the tiniest part in making *Blind Spot* happen that you helped my dream come true. Thank you, from the bottom of my heart.

About the Author

Maud Rowell is a freelance writer and translator based in London. After a year spent travelling and working in South Korea, Japan, and Taiwan, she read Japanese Studies at the University of Cambridge and then attained a Masters degree in magazine journalism. She was diagnosed with a degenerative sight condition aged 19 in a Seoul hospital, and since then has used her writing to explore and educate others on the topic of blindness, often through the lens of art and art history.

In 2021, she won the Holman Prize, an annual $25,000 grant offered by the San Francisco Lighthouse for the Blind and Visually Impaired, enabling her to embark on a year-long trip around some of Japan's most remote parts, and then write and illustrate a book about her travels. She sets off in April 2022.

Hobbies include reading multilingual and experimental fiction, film photography – processed in the makeshift darkroom built by her father at home – and creative writing, in both Japanese and English.

Instagram: @maud.rowell

Twitter: @maud_rowell

About the Inklings series

This book is part of 404 Ink's Inkling series which presents big ideas in pocket-sized books.
They are all available at 404ink.com/shop

If you enjoyed this book, you may also enjoy these titles in the series:

The Appendix: Transmasculine Joy in a Transphobic Culture – Liam Konemann

 In 2019, Liam Konemann began collating what he called 'The Appendix', a simple record of ongoing transphobia in the UK that he came across in day-to-day life: from the flippant comments of peers to calculated articles and reviews in newspapers. When the list began to take its toll on his mental health, he changed tack by asking different questions: how is beauty in transmasculinity found? And how is it maintained in a transphobic world?

The New University: Local Solutions to a Global Crisis – James Coe

The New University considers the enormous challenge of reimagining how our public realm can function in a post-COVID landscape, and the institutions that form an indelible part of our civic life. Coe reimagines the University as a more civic and personal institution, believing we can get there through realigning our research to communal benefit.

No Man's Land: Living Between Two Cultures – Anne East

In *No Man's Land*, Anne explores this chasm in more detail, how it is to feel one thing and yet be perceived as another. What are the emotions that people feel in this limbo? Why is culture so important? And how does it feel to experience that cultural no man's land? A book on acceptance and shining a light on the cultural vacuum that exists for many, this is a must read from a voice rarely heard.